# Grammar Dimensions
## Workbook One

## Cheryl Benz
*Miami-Dade Community College*

Heinle & Heinle Publishers

 An International Thomson Publishing Company

Pacific Grove • Albany • Bonn • Boston • Cincinnati • Detroit • London
Madrid • Melbourne • Mexico City • New York • Paris
San Francisco • Tokyo • Toronto • Washington

**Photos on:** page 1 and 44, courtesy of Pat Martin; page 54, courtesy of H. Armstrong Roberts.

ISBN 08384-4001-0

10 9 8 7 6 5 4 3 2

# Grammar Dimensions

*Workbook One*

# Contents

# UNIT

## 1

# The Verb Be
## Affirmative Statements, Subject Pronouns

**EXERCISE 1** (*Focus 1*)

My name is Juan.
I'm from Mexico.
I am 19.
I'm single.
I'm a student.

I'm Julia.
I'm German.
I'm 19.
I'm single.
I'm a student.

My name is Rosa.
I'm Puerto Rican.
I'm 35 years old.
I'm divorced.
I am a teacher.

I'm Yumiko
I'm from Japan.
I'm 35.
I'm married.
I'm an engineer.

**Put the sentence in the correct order.**

EXAMPLE:   are/ Juan and Rosa/ Hispanic.   *Juan and Rosa are Hispanic.*

**1.** divorced. / is / Rosa _____

**2.** Yumiko / Japanese. / is _____

**3.** are / single. / Juan and Julia _____

**4.** 35. / The engineer / is _____

**5.** is / The German / a student. _____

**6.** from Puerto Rico. / The teacher / is _____

**7.** Juan and Julia / 19 years old. / are _____

**8.** a student. / is / The Mexican _____

**9.** Asian. / Yumiko / is _____

**10.** are / single. / The students _____

## EXERCISE 2  (Focus 1)

**Fill in the blanks with *is* or *are*.**

EXAMPLE:   The students __*are*__ 19 years old.

1. Yumiko _____ Japanese.
2. Rosa _____ a teacher.
3. The engineer _____ Japanese.
4. Yumiko and Rosa _____ 35.
5. The students _____ 19 years old.


## EXERCISE 3  (Focus 2)

**Replace the noun phrase with a subject pronoun.**

EXAMPLE:   Julia is German. __*She*__ is a student.

1. Julia is from Europe. _____ is German.
2. Juan and Julia are 19 years old. _____ are single.
3. Rosa is from Puerto Rico. _____ is a teacher.
4. The student is 19 years old. _____ is Mexican.
5. Japan is a country. _____ is in Asia.
6. My name is Yumiko. _____ am Japanese.
7. You and I are from Asia. _____ are Asians.
8. Mexico is a country. _____ is in North America.
9. Juan is from Mexico. _____ is single.
10. Rosa is a teacher. _____ is divorced.

Write three sentences about yourself using *be*. Then write three sentences about a partner.

EXAMPLE: *I'm from Brazil.*

**YOU**

1. _____

_____

2. _____

_____

3. _____

_____

**PARTNER**

1. _____

_____

2. _____

_____

3. _____

_____

**EXERCISE 5** (*Focus 3*)

Rewrite the sentence using contractions (subject pronoun + *be*).

EXAMPLE: Juan is Hispanic. *He's Hispanic.*

1. Julia and Juan are single. _____

2. Julia is a student. _____

3. Rosa is from Puerto Rico. _____

4. Yumiko is an engineer from Japan. _____

5. Mexico and the United States are in North America. _____

6. My name is Julia. I am European. _____

7. Julia and I are students. _____

8. Julia and Rosa are single. _____

9. Yumiko is 35 years old. _____

10. Juan is a student from Mexico. _____

## EXERCISE 6　(*Focus 4*)

1. **Ask your partner the following questions:**

   **a.** What's your name?

   **b.** Where are you from?

   **c.** How are you?

2. **Introduce your partner to the other people in your class.**

## EXERCISE 7　(*Focus 4*)

**Think about the correct way to greet the people below. Write *formal* if the greeting should be formal. Write *informal* if the greeting can be informal. Act out the greetings with a partner.**

1. your teacher _____

2. your mother _____

3. a classmate _____

4. a young child _____

5. a doctor _____

6. a police officer _____

# UNIT 2

## The Verb Be

### Yes/No Questions, Be + Adjective, Negative Statements

Fill in the blanks below. Then choose the correct answer to the puzzle.

### GUESS THE PLACE

_____ this place in Europe?

Yes, _____ _____.

_____ _____ in Switzerland?

No, _____ _____.

_____ _____ in France?

_____, it is.

_____ _____ a museum?

Yes, _____ _____.

_____ _____ in Paris?

Yes, _____ _____.

Is it _____ ?

(the Hermitage, the Louvre)

### GUESS THE FAMOUS COUPLE

Are we married?

_____, you aren't.

_____ _____ from the United States?

No, _____ _____.

_____ _____ from Great Britain?

Yes, _____ _____.

_____ _____ part of the royal family?

_____, you are.

Are we _____?

(Charles and Diana, Bill and Hillary)

### GUESS WHO I AM

Am I female?

No, _____ _____.

_____ _____ an actor?

_____, you aren't.

_____ _____ a singer?

No, _____ _____.

_____ _____ an athlete?

_____ you are.

_____ _____ soccer player?

Yes, _____ _____.

_____ _____ from Brazil?

Yes, you are.

Am I _____?

(Pele, Michael Jordan)

## EXERCISE 2   (Focus 1 )

Imagine that you are a famous person. Your partner must guess who you are by asking Yes or No questions.

EXAMPLE:   **A:** *Are you an actress?*

**B:** *Yes, I am.*

**A:** *Are you an American?*

**B:** *No, I'm not...*

## EXERCISE 3   (Focus 2)

| busy | good | sick | healthy | ugly | young |
|------|------|------|---------|------|-------|
| angry | energetic | funny | overweight | strong | tall |
| happy | beautiful | poor | serious | weak | sad |
| thin | messy | rich | intelligent | loud | noisy |
| athletic | frightened | shy | outgoing | quiet | tired |
| organized | interesting | short | talkative | neat | calm |
| nervous | homesick | handsome | friendly | lonely | old |

### PART A

Write five sentences describing yourself. Use the list of adjectives to help you.

EXAMPLE:   <u>I am outgoing.</u>

1. _____
2. _____
3. _____
4. _____
5. _____

### PART B

Using the same list, write five sentences about your parents.

EXAMPLE:   <u>My parents are happy.</u>

1. _____
2. _____
3. _____
4. _____
5. _____

## PART C

**Using the same list, write five sentences about someone else in your family.**

EXAMPLE:   My uncle is athletic.

1. _____
2. _____
3. _____
4. _____
5. _____

## EXERCISE 4   (Focuses 1 and 2)

**Share some of the sentences you wrote in Exercise 3 with a partner. Ask Yes or No questions about the people your partner describes.**

EXAMPLE:   **A:** My uncle is athletic.

**B:** Is he a basketball player?

**A:** No he isn't; he is a tennis player.

## EXERCISE 5   (Focus 3)

**Using the list of adjectives from Exercise 3, write five _negative_ statements about yourself. Share the statements with your partner.**

EXAMPLE:   I am not neat.

1. _____
2. _____
3. _____
4. _____
5. _____

**Write sentences describing the picture using the cues and negative statements. Follow the example.**

    2 + 2 = ?

EXAMPLE:   short building / tall   _The building isn't short. It's tall._

1. small mouse / big _____
   _____

2. boring speaker / interesting _____
   _____

3. crying baby / quiet _____
   _____

4. fat Santa / thin _____
   _____

5. old woman / young _____
   _____

6. handsome man / ugly _____
   _____

7. soft toy / hard _____
   _____

8. busy bees / lazy _____
   _____

9. difficult problem / easy _____
   _____

10. awake children / tired _____
    _____

# UNIT 3 The Verb Be
## Wh-Question Words, Prepositions of location

**EXERCISE 1** (*Focus 1*)

Complete the story by filling in each blank with the correct question word and the form of *be*. The first one has been done for you as an example.

**Monte:** Welcome to the "64-Cent Question," the game show where we ask easy questions and the contestants can win up to 64 cents. I'm your host Monte Money and our two contestants tonight are Feliz Happy and Sandy Beach.

**Monte:** <u>How are</u> you tonight, Feliz?

**Feliz:** I'm just happy to be here, Monte.

**Monte:** Great, and _____ _____ you, Sandy?

**Sandy:** Fine, thank you, Monte.

**Monte:** Great, now let's begin tonight's game. The first question is for you Feliz. _____ _____ the capital of the United States?

**Feliz:** Washington, D.C.

**Monte:** Right! Now, for you Sandy. _____ _____ the director of the movie ET?

**Sandy:** Stephen Spielberg.

**Monte:** Great! Now Feliz, _____ _____ plants green?

**Feliz:** Because they contain chlorophyll.

**Monte:** You've got it. Sandy, _____ _____ _____ the pyramids in Egypt?

**Sandy:** About 4,700 years old.

**Monte:** Correct! Feliz, _____ _____ the first day of spring?

**Feliz:** March 21.

**Monte:** Right again! Now, Sandy. _____ _____ is Leonardo da Vinci's painting commonly called the *Mona Lisa*?

**Sandy:** In the Louvre in Paris.

**Monte:** Yes! For you, Feliz, _____ _____ seven times eight?

**Feliz:** Fifty-six.

**Monte:** You're right again. Sandy, _____ _____ the author of *Tom Sawyer*?

**Sandy:** Mark Twain.

**Monte:** Okay. Feliz, _____ _____ the Statue of Liberty located?

**Feliz:** In New York.

**Monte:** Finally, for you, Sandy, the last question. _____ _____ Thanksgiving celebrated in the United States?

**Sandy:** On the fourth Thursday in November.

**Monte:** Amazing, folks! We have a tie! Well, tune in next week for the "64-Cent Question!"


## EXERCISE 2    (Focus 2)

This is an information gap activity. With a partner, take turns asking each other word meanings. One of you covers up the answers in Part A, and asks the other for meanings and sample sentences for the first five words. The answers are in Part B. Then switch, using the words in Part B, whose answers you covered in Part A.

## PART A

1. banjo _____

_____

2. talkative _____

_____

3. lumberjack _____

_____

4. fog _____

_____

5. sailor _____

_____

1. chubby:  _(adjective) round and fat—The little boy had a chubby face._
2. dye: _(verb) to change the color—She dyes her hair._
3. hail: _(noun) small round pieces of frozen rain—The hail destroyed the plants._
4. ignore: _(verb). to pay no attention to—He ignores his mother when she tells him to clean his room._
5. pretend: _(verb) to imagine; to make believe. I like to pretend I'm a clown._

## PART B

1. hail _____
   _____

2. pretend _____
   _____

3. ignore _____
   _____

4. chubby _____
   _____

5. dye_____
   _____

1. banjo:  (noun) a musical instrument with a round body and five strings—The musician played her banjo.

2. fog:  (noun) clouds that reach to the ground—I could hardly see through the fog.

3. lumberjack:  (noun) a person who cuts down trees—The lumberjack cut down the giant tree.

4. sailor:  (noun) a person who works on a boat or ship—The sailor turned the ship into the wind.

5. talkative:  (adjective) talking a lot—That talkative lady doesn't let anyone else say a word.

## EXERCISE 3    (Focus 3)

**Answer the questions using the information on the map.**

1. How's the weather in Miami today? _____

_____

2. What's the temperature in Chicago? _____

_____

3. How's the weather in Seattle? _____

_____

4. What's the temperature in New York? _____

_____

5. How's the weather in Los Angeles?_____

_____

6. How's the weather in San Antonio? _____

_____

7. What's the temperature in Cleveland? _____

_____

8. How's the weather in Billings?_____

_____

9. How's the weather in Albuquerque? _____

_____

10. What's the temperature in Baton Rogue?_____

_____

**EXERCISE 4**    (*Focus 3*)

Find the weather map in today's newspaper. Take turns asking your partner questions about the weather in different U.S. cities.

**EXERCISE 5**    (*Focus 4*)

Look at this map of the time zones of Europe and answer the questions.

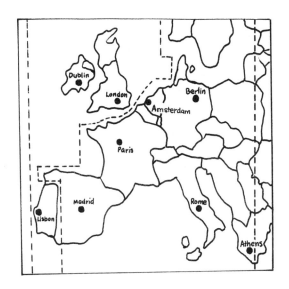

1. It's 7 A.M. in London. What time is it in Paris? _____

2. It's 9 A.M. in Lisbon. What time is it in Berlin? _____

3. It's 11 A.M. in Rome. What time is it in Madrid? _____

4. It's 10 A.M. in Dublin. What time is it in Amsterdam? _____

5. It's 11 A.M. in London  What time is it in Rome? _____

**Write five more questions using this pattern. Ask your partner for the answers.**

1. _____

_____

2. _____

_____

3. _____

_____

4. _____

_____

5. _____

_____

Draw these figures according to the directions. Then write a sentence about each figure using the verb *to be* and a prepositional phrase. The first one has been done for you as an example.

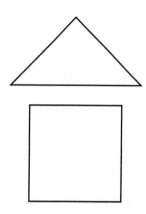

1. Draw a square.

1. _The square is under the triangle._
   _____

2. Draw a triangle above the square.

2. _____
   _____

3. Draw two rectangles under the square.

3. _____
   _____

4. Draw a face on the square.

4. _____
   _____

5. Draw a circle behind the square.

5. _____
   _____

1. Draw a circle.

1. _____
   _____

2. Draw another circle next to the first circle.

2. _____
   _____

3. Draw a line between the circles.

3. _____
   _____

4. Draw a square in the circles.

4. _____
   _____

5. Draw two triangles opposite each circle.

5. _____
   _____

1. Draw a man.

1. _____
   _____

2. Draw a woman near the man.

2. _____
   _____

3. Draw a boy in front of the man.

3. _____
   _____

4. Draw a girl between the man and the woman.

4. _____
   _____

5. Draw a house behind the people.

5. _____
   _____

Draw a simple picture, but don't show it to your partner. Tell your partner how to draw the picture using the verb *to be* and a prepositional, and then compare the two pictures.

Using *where are* or *where is*, write a question about the location of each cue word. Then answer your questions with the help of the picture. Follow the example.

EXAMPLE: towels _Where are the towels? On the dresser._

1. keys _____
_____

2. shirt _____
_____

3. pants _____
_____

4. books _____
_____

5. shoes _____
_____

6. sweater _____
_____

7. jewelry _____
_____

8. glasses _____
_____

9. pillow _____
_____

10. brush _____
_____

# TOEFL®

## Test Preparation Exercises
### Units 1–3

**Choose the *one* word or phrase that best completes each sentence.**

1. The students _____ from Mexico.
   - (A) and
   - (B) be
   - (C) are
   - (D) is

2. When _____?
   - (A) time is it
   - (B) is your vacation
   - (C) is Canada
   - (D) old are you

3. _____ is married.
   - (A) They
   - (B) It
   - (C) We
   - (D) She

4. _____ students in level 1.
   - (A) She is
   - (B) It is
   - (C) They are
   - (D) I am

5. _____? It means very big.
   - (A) What means huge
   - (B) What is the spelling of huge
   - (C) What is the meaning of huge
   - (D) What is the pronunciation of huge

6. _____ shy and athletic.
   - (A) She's
   - (B) It isn't
   - (C) Am
   - (D) It's

7. The student _____ Japanese.
   - (A) is
   - (B) am
   - (C) be
   - (D) she

8. _____ an English teacher.
   - (A) They are
   - (B) I'm
   - (C) They're
   - (D) To be

9. _____ Montreal? _____ in Quebec.
   - (A) Where is...It's
   - (B) Where be...It is
   - (C) Where is...Is
   - (D) When is...It's

10. Dr. Martin is _____.
        (A) opens                     (C) school
        (B) busy                      (D) yes

11. You _____ short.
        (A) it's                       (C) no
        (B) am                       (D) aren't

12. _____? I'm 35.
        (A) How age are you       (C) How old you are
        (B) How are you          (D) How old are you

13. _____ am not short.
        (A) I                        (C) You
        (B) We're                    (D) I'm

14. A: Hi! I'm Anne Parker.
    B: _____.
        (A) Nice to you meet, Ms. Parker   (C) Is nice, Anne.
        (B) Nice to meet you, Ms. Anne    (D) Nice to meet you, Anne.

15. _____ your teacher?
        (A) Who                    (C) Who's
        (B) Who are               (D) Whose

**Identify the *one* underlined word or phrase that must be changed for the sentence to be grammatically correct.**

16. Is it cold? What's the temperature today? It has 30 degrees.
     A        B          C                D

17. Is Jose from China? No, Jose's no from China.
     A                 B    C  D

18. Tense I am? Yes, you are; try to relax.
     A         B    C       D

19. Who is your teacher? Ms. Betty is my teacher.
     A        B          C        D

20. How are those problems? He isn't difficult.
     A       B           C      D

21. Are you single? Yes, I'm.
     A     B       C  D

22. Is it raining? No, is not. It's sunny.
     A  B       C       D

**23.** <u>What time</u> <u>it is</u>? <u>It's three o'clock</u> <u>in the afternoon</u>.
           **A**      **B**         **C**               **D**

**24.** <u>How's</u> <u>the weather today</u>? <u>Is</u> <u>cool and rainy</u>.
       **A**            **B**        **C**      **D**

**25.** <u>When</u> <u>are you wet</u>? <u>I'm wet</u> because of <u>the rain</u>.
       **A**        **B**        **C**              **D**

# Nouns

## Count and Noncount nouns, Be + Adjective + Noun

**EXERCISE 1** *(Focus 1)*

Look at the underlined nouns and circle all noncount nouns. The first one has been done for you as an example.

(Chicken) is a kind of <u>meat</u>.

<u>Chickens</u> are birds with <u>wings</u> and <u>feathers</u>.

1. Is there <u>money</u> in the <u>jar</u>?

2. Yes, there is some <u>change</u>.

3. Is there a <u>quarter</u> in the jar?

4. No, but I think there are two <u>dimes</u> and a <u>nickel</u>.

5. His <u>clothing</u> is old.

6. His <u>pants</u> are torn.

7. His <u>shirt</u> is dirty.

Put each word below in its correct category. Write *a* or *an* in front of each word.

| | | | | |
|---|---|---|---|---|
| tie | month | potato | blouse | helicopter |
| day | carrot | airplane | radish | undershirt |
| pea | sweater | truck | uniform | automobile |
| herb | year | week | train | hour |

| CLOTHES | TRANSPORTATION | VEGETABLES | TIME |
|---|---|---|---|
| 1. | 1. | 1. | 1. |
| 2. | 2. | 2. | 2. |
| 3. | 3. | 3. | 3. |
| 4. | 4. | 4. | 4. |
| 5. | 5. | 5. | 5. |

**EXERCISE 3**  (*Focus 3*)

Complete the story by filling in each blank with the correct plural form of each word below. The first letter of each word is given to help you. The first one has been done for you as an example.

| | | | | | |
|---|---|---|---|---|---|
| princess | toy | witch | monster | candy | hero |
| girl | class | bat | country | holiday | knife |
| cat | party | door | baby | ax | orange |
| fairy | story | wish | treat | boy | trick |
| house | | | | | |

### Halloween in the United States

It is interesting to learn about h <u>olidays</u> in different c_____. Halloween is celebrated on October 31 in the United States. Small children and even b_____ wear costumes. Some children like frightening costumes. They dress like w_____ and m_____. The scary costumes can include plastic k_____ and a_____ with fake blood, but their weapons don't really hurt

anyone. Some b_____ dress like Superman and Batman and other h_____.
F_____ that give people w_____ or Cinderella and Sleeping Beauty and
other p_____ from s_____ are popular costumes for g_____.
Still other children dress like c_____, b_____, and other animals. In the
afternoon the children have p_____ in their c_____ at school. When it gets
dark, the children knock on all the d_____ the h_____ in their neighborhood.
The people in the houses give the children t_____ like c_____,
o_____ and other fruit, and small t_____. If they don't receive treats,
some children play t_____.


**EXERCISE 4**   (*Focus 4*)

Listen to your teacher read the regular plural nouns you used in Exercise 3. Write
each word in the correct category according to its pronunciation. The first one has been
done for you as an example.

| /z/ | /s/ | /iz/ |
|---|---|---|
| holidays | | |


**EXERCISE 5**   (*Focus 4*)

Practice saying each of the words in the lists you made in Exercise 4. Use a tape
recorder if possible to check your pronunciation.

## EXERCISE 6    (Focus 5)

DUANE GILLOGLY

Write the irregular plural form of each of the following nouns in the correct category. Use a dictionary to look up words you do not know how to spell. The first one has been done for you as an example.

| Nouns | man | fish | child |
|---|---|---|---|
| person | woman | ox | deer |
| foot | deer | goose | hoof |
| moose | tooth | mouse | hair |

| HUMANS | ANIMALS | BODY PARTS |
|---|---|---|
| people | | |

## EXERCISE 7    (Focus 6)

Circle the mistakes in count and noncount nouns in the following paragraphs. Correct the mistakes and then rewrite the paragraphs. The first sentence has been done for you as an example.

Informations are easier to get with today's new technology. A news is transmitted around the world by TV satellites. Computers also make informations easier to get. Computers can help a person do his homeworks. Computer networks allow people to tell some news and give some advices. With computer mails a person can send a message with an electricity and a phone line.

*Information is easier to get with today's new technology.*

_____

_____

_____

_____

_____

_____

_____

_____

_____

_____

There is a new kind of store in the United States now. Superstores are a combination of supermarkets and discount stores. Superstores have everything from foods to furnitures. At a superstore you can buy beverages like a coffee, a tea, or a milk. In the same store you can buy jewelerys, clothings, musics, and luggages. You can also buy things like a bread, a rice, a sugar, or a fruit. You should bring lots of moneys with you when you go to a superstore because there is a lot to buy. But one thing you can't buy at a superstore is the love.

_____

_____

_____

_____

_____

_____

_____

_____

_____

_____

This is an information gap activity. Work with a partner; one of you will look at Picture A while the other looks at Picture B. You will learn some of the prices of the items for sale in the Bag and Save grocery store while your partner learns other prices. Take turns asking each other the prices of the missing items.

Picture A

EXAMPLE:    *How much are eggs?* [$.89 per dozen.]

Use the pictures from Exercise 8 to take turns with your partner asking each other the price of more than one pound or item.

Picture B

EXAMPLE:    *How much for two cans of peaches?* [$1.98.]

**Write sentences about your country using the *be* + adjective + noun pattern. Share the information about your country with your classmates.**

EXAMPLE: popular sport

*Soccer is a popular sport in Brazil.*

1. popular sport

2. famous person

3. historic building

4. crowded city

5. delicious food

6. beautiful place to visit

7. popular actress

8. exciting holiday

9. expensive car

10. traditional musical instrument

# UNIT 5

# The Verb *Have*

Affirmative and Negative Statements,
Questions and Short Answers,
*Some/Any*

<hr />

**EXERCISE 1**    (*Focus 1*)

This is the Yohnson family from Wisconsin. Yan Yohnson, his wife, Yill, and their son,
Yack, have many things for the cold and snowy Wisconsin winters.

This is the Sunshine family from California. Ray Sunshine and his wife, Tawny, and their daughter, Malibu, have many things for the warm California weather.

Using the cues, write sentences about what each family has.

EXAMPLE:  sled ___Yack Yohnson has a sled.___

house ___Both families have a house.___

barbecue ___The Sunshine family has a barbecue.___

**1.** pet _____

_____

**2.** warm coat _____

_____

**3.** snow shovel _____

_____

**4.** hammock _____

_____

**5.** swimming pool _____

_____

**6.** porch _____

_____

**7.** child _____

_____

**8.** daughter _____

_____

**9.** son _____

_____

**10.** palm trees _____

_____

**11.** fireplace _____

_____

**12.** air conditioner _____

_____

**13.** woodpile _____

_____

**14.** scarf _____

_____

**15.** wife _____

_____

**16.** sunglasses _____

_____

## EXERCISE 2 (Focus 2)

**Use the pictures from Exercise 1 to complete the following sentences with true statements using the negative form of *have*. Follow the example.**

EXAMPLE: Yan Yohnson ___*Yan Yohnson doesn't have a daughter.*___

**1.** Ray Sunshine _____

_____

**2.** The Yohnson family _____

_____

**3.** Yan and Yill Yohnson _____

_____

**4.** The Sunshine's house _____

_____

**5.** Yack Yohnson _____

_____

**6.** The dog _____

_____

**7.** Malibu _____

_____

**8.** The swimming pool _____

_____

**9.** The cat _____

_____

**10.** Tawny Sunshine _____

_____


## EXERCISE 3　(Focus 3)

**With three classmates, take turns asking who has the following items in their homes. Record the short answers on the chart below.**

|  | NAME | NAME | NAME |
|---|---|---|---|
|  | _____ | _____ | _____ |

**DO YOU HAVE...**

|  | | | |
|---|---|---|---|
| **1.** children? | _____ | _____ | _____ |
| **2.** a TV? | _____ | _____ | _____ |
| **3.** a car? | _____ | _____ | _____ |
| **4.** a tent? | _____ | _____ | _____ |
| **5.** a jet plane? | _____ | _____ | _____ |
| **6.** a snow shovel? | _____ | _____ | _____ |
| **7.** a watch? | _____ | _____ | _____ |
| **8.** a sister? | _____ | _____ | _____ |
| **9.** chopsticks? | _____ | _____ | _____ |
| **10.** a swimming pool? | _____ | _____ | _____ |

**Using the information from the pictures on pages 28 and 29, write the questions that go with the following answers.**

EXAMPLE:    Does Ray Sunshine have a son?

No, he doesn't have a son.

1. _____

Yes, they have a swimming pool.

2. _____

Yes, he has a sled.

3. _____

No, they don't have a fireplace.

4. _____

Yes, she has a cat.

5. _____

Yes, they have a fireplace.

6. _____

No, they don't have a wood pile.

7. _____

Yes, California has palm trees.

8. _____

No, Wisconsin doesn't have palm trees.

9. _____

Yes, they have a hammock.

10. _____

Yes, Yack has a warm coat.

11. _____

Yes, she has sunglasses.

Fill in each blank in the conversation with *some* or *any*. The first one has been done for you as an example.

**Kay:** What are you doing this weekend?

**Ray:** I don't know. I have **(1)** _____some_____ free time and I want to go to the movies, but I don't have **(2)** _____ money.

**Kay:** Doesn't your father have **(3)** _____ money that he could lend you?

**Ray:** He has money but he doesn't lend **(4)** _____ of it to me. He says that if I want **(5)** _____ money I have to work for it. I don't want to do **(6)** _____ work. I just want to have **(7)** _____ fun.

**Kay:** Doing **(8)** _____ work is not that hard. If you mow a couple of lawns you can make **(9)** _____ money fast.

**Ray:** I guess that isn't so difficult. Besides, I won't have **(10)** _____ fun if I stay home all weekend.

**EXERCISE 6** (Focus 5)

Write a complete sentence, using the polite requests, for each cue.

EXAMPLE: books

_Excuse me, do you have any books?_ _____

1. pencils _____

_____

2. telephone _____

_____

3. fountain pens _____

_____

4. basketballs _____

_____

5. restrooms _____

_____

6. photocopier _____

_____

7. Ashland University t-shirts _____

_____

**8.** notebooks _____

_____

**9.** computer disks _____

_____

**10.** comic books _____

_____


**EXERCISE 7**    (*Focus 5*)

Look at the picture of the Ashland University bookstore. Using the requests in Exercise 6, take turns with your partner role-playing a customer and a salesclerk in the bookstore. The salesclerk should answer the polite requests according to what he or she can see in the picture.

**EXERCISE 8**    (*Focus 6*)

Use the pictures of the Yohnson and Sunshine families from Exercise 1 on pages 28 and 29 to write three sentences describing each person in the pictures. Use the verb *be* in one sentence in each group and the verb *have* in two sentences.

EXAMPLE:    The Yohnsons

_The Yohnsons are short._____

_The Yohnsons have black hair._____

_They have bangs._____

## YAN YOHNSON

1. _____
   _____
2. _____
   _____
3. _____
   _____

## YILL YOHNSON

1. _____
   _____
2. _____
   _____
3. _____
   _____

## YACK YOHNSON

1. _____
   _____
2. _____
   _____
3. _____
   _____

## THE SUNSHINES

1. _____
   _____
2. _____
   _____
3. _____
   _____

## RAY SUNSHINE

1. _____
   _____
2. _____
   _____
3. _____
   _____

## TAWNY SUNSHINE

1. _____
   _____
2. _____
   _____
3. _____
   _____

## MALIBU SUNSHINE

1. _____
   _____
2. _____
   _____
3. _____
   _____

# UNIT
# 6 This/That/These/Those
## Possessives

**EXERCISE 1** (*Focus 1*)

Look at the pages from these two different catalogues. Complete the sentences below using the correct demonstrative pronouns and the correct form of the verb *be*.

EXAMPLE: ___Those___ ___are___ shoes.

1. _____ _____ a straw hat.
2. _____ _____ a thick sweater.
3. _____ _____ a cowboy hat.
4. _____ _____ short pants.
5. _____ _____ a polka-dot dress.
6. _____ _____ shoes.
7. _____ _____ an expensive sweater.
8. _____ _____ long pants.
9. _____ _____ a necklace.
10. _____ _____ a bracelet.
11. _____ _____ a striped shirt.

**Write questions using demonstratives for the nouns below. Then answer the questions. Use the words in the box below as clues.**

EXAMPLE: near the speaker: newspapers, magazines

*What are these?*

*These are things to read.*

1. far from the speaker: couch, bed _____

_____

2. near the speaker: chicken, beef _____

_____

3. far from the speaker: doll _____

_____

4. near the speaker: boy, girl _____

_____

5. far from the speaker: green, yellow _____

_____

6. near the speaker: pine, maple _____

_____

7. near the speaker: aunt _____

_____

8. far from the speaker: apartment, house _____

_____

9. near the speaker: can opener, toaster _____

_____

10. near the speaker: blanket _____

_____

| | | | |
|---|---|---|---|
| ~~things to read~~ | toy | children | furniture |
| kitchen machines | trees | relative | bedding |
| places to live | meat | colors | |

## EXERCISE 3    (*Focus 3*)

**For each picture choose the correct caption and write it under the picture. The first one has been done for you as an example.**

1. Mark's computer is new.

2. Erle's homework is incomplete.

3. Maya's car is a compact.

4. Mexico's flag has an eagle and a snake on it.

5. Monique's car is luxurious.

6. Paulo's homework is finished.

7. James' computer is old.

8. The secretaries' desks are neat.

9. Canada's flag has a maple leaf on it.

10. The secretaries' desks are messy.

Maya's car is a compact.

_____

_____

_____

_____

_____

_____

_____

_____

_____

_____

_____

_____
_____
_____
_____

_____
_____
_____
_____

_____
_____
_____
_____

_____
_____
_____
_____

_____
_____
_____
_____

_____
_____
_____
_____

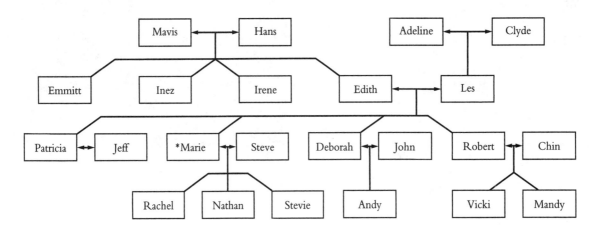

**Write a sentence describing Marie's relationship with each person below.**

EXAMPLE:   Nathan: ___Nathan is Marie's son._____

1. Mandy _____

2. Mavis _____

3. Emmitt _____

4. Steve _____

5. Andy _____

6. Les _____

7. Rachel _____

8. Stevie _____

9. Hans _____

10. Chin _____

11. Jeff _____

12. Adeline and Clyde _____

13. Irene _____

14. Vicki _____

Fill in the blanks below to show your own family tree.

**My Family Tree**

| _____ | _____ | _____ | _____ |
| Grandfather | Grandmother | Grandfather | Grandmother |

| _____ | | _____ |
| Mother | | Father |

_____
Me

**Answer the following questions about your family tree using complete sentences.**

1. What is your mother's name?_____

_____

2. What is your father's name? _____

_____

3. What are your grandmothers' names? _____

_____

4. What are your grandfathers' names?_____

_____

**EXERCISE 6** (*Focus 4*)

Sun and Lee Park are brothers from Korea. They are studying English in the United States, but they are studying at different schools and in different programs. Sun is studying at a community college. Lee is studying in the intensive language program at a university. The brothers are talking on the phone and comparing the two different English programs.

**Complete the dialogue using the correct possessive adjectives. The first one has been done for you as an example.**

**Sun:** Hello, Lee. How are you? How is _____*your*_____ English program?

**Lee:** It's great. I have small classes. _____ classes only have 10 students.

**Sun:** That's good. _____ classes are very crowded. I have 30 students in my classes.

**Lee:** Does your program have a lab? We have a language lab. _____ lab has computers, tape recorders, and listening stations.

**Sun:** Yes, we have several labs. The computer lab is very large and _____ computers are all new.

**Lee:** What about your teacher?

**Sun:** She is very nice. _____ name is Mrs. Nation. She always encourages us. She tells us _____ English is improving every day.

**Lee:** _____ teacher is a man. _____ name is Mr. Bahamonde. He also encourages us, but _____ tests are very difficult. He makes us work very hard. What about a textbook? Which book are you using?

**Sun:** We're using *Grammar Dimensions*. It's a very good book and the activities are fun.

**Lee:** We're using *Grammar Dimensions* too. I like it. How much does _____ program cost?

**Sun:** It's not too expensive.

**Lee:** _____ program is expensive. _____ cost is high and I don't have any time to work.

**Sun:** You should try _____ program. It is only part-time.


## EXERCISE 7    (*Focus 4*)

Find one or two people in your class that fit the following descriptions. Write his/her/their name(s) on the lines at the right.

| DESCRIPTION | NAMES |
|---|---|
| 1. Her eyes are dark. | _____ |
| | _____ |
| 2. His legs are long. | _____ |
| | _____ |
| 3. Their ears are small. | _____ |
| | _____ |
| 4. His hair is long. | _____ |
| | _____ |
| 5. Her fingers are long. | _____ |

Complete the last five descriptions with your own words. Share your answers with your classmates.

6. Their hands are _____       _____

_____.       _____

**7.** Our arms are _____    _____

_____.    _____

**8.** My nose is _____    _____

_____.    _____

**9.** Our _____    _____

_____.    _____

**10.** My _____    _____

_____.    _____

## EXERCISE 8    (*Focus 4*)

Match the people with their things. Then write a statement using the correct possessive pronoun.

| | |
|---|---|
| **1.** Lucy is an accountant. | **A.** a book bag |
| **2.** Billy is a truck driver. | **B.** a calculator |
| **3.** Rudolfo and Juan are firemen. | **C.** a cash register |
| **4.** Scott is a plumber. | **D.** a fire hose |
| **5.** Toni is a singer. | **E.** a dog leash |
| **6.** Joyce is a dog trainer. | **F.** police badges |
| **7.** Julia and Thomas are police officers. | **G.** plans for a house |
| **8.** Angie is a student. | **H.** music |
| **9.** Roy is a salesclerk. | **I.** a truck |
| **10.** Isaac is an architect. | **J.** a football |
| **11.** Bruce is a football player. | **K.** a wrench |

**1.** _____Lucy is an accountant. The calculator is hers._____

**2.** _____

**3.** _____

**4.** _____

**5.** _____

**6.** _____

**7.** _____

8. _____

9. _____

10. _____

11. _____


**EXERCISE 9**　(*Focus 5*)

The objects listed below belong to the people in the pictures. Using *Whose...?*, write questions to determine owners. Then write two answers, one with the possessive noun and one with the possessive pronoun.

James

Ashley

Ginette and Jasmine

EXAMPLE:　false teeth

_Whose false teeth are these?_　_They're James' false teeth._

_____　_They're his._

1. mother _____

_____

2. notebooks _____

_____

3. boyfriends _____

_____

4. rocking chair _____

_____

5. false teeth _____

_____

6. bottle _____

_____

**7.** cane _____

_____

**8.** tape players _____

_____

**9.** toy _____

_____

**10.** cassette tapes _____

_____

**11.** glasses _____

_____

**12.** diaper _____

_____

# TOEFL®

# Test Preparation Exercises
## Units 4–6

**Choose the *one* word or phrase that best completes each sentence.**

1. The teacher _____ problem.
    - (A) has a
    - (B) has any
    - (C) be a
    - (D) have any

2. She works at an older school. They don't have computers at _____ school.
    - (A) this
    - (B) that
    - (C) these
    - (D) those

3. What's _____? It's _____ airplane.
    - (A) these...an
    - (B) these...a
    - (C) that...an
    - (D) that...some

4. She doesn't _____ new book.
    - (A) has a
    - (B) have an
    - (C) has an
    - (D) have a

5. Costa Rica and Brazil are _____.
    - (A) countrys
    - (B) a country
    - (C) country
    - (D) countries

6. I _____ children.
    - (A) no have any
    - (B) don't have some
    - (C) don't have any
    - (D) doesn't has any

7. He has _____ homework in _____ class.
    - (A) a...that
    - (B) one...these
    - (C) any...that
    - (D) some...that

8. Do the children _____ toys? Yes, they do. The _____ are new.
    - (A) has any...children's toys
    - (B) have any...children's toys
    - (C) has a...children's toy
    - (D) have any...children't toys

9. Ulrika _____ children.
    - (A) has one
    - (B) has two
    - (C) have some
    - (D) have any

10. They _____ bread.
    (A) have a
    (B) has some
    (C) have any
    (D) have some

11. _____ short brown hair.
    (A) That girl no has
    (B) Those girls doesn't have
    (C) The girl doesn't has
    (D) That girl doesn't have

12. There are two _____.
    (A) deer
    (B) deers
    (C) mans
    (D) man

13. I have _____ sugar. There isn't _____ more.
    (A) some…any
    (B) some…some
    (C) no…any
    (D) a…some

14. Do the dogs have food? No, the _____ are empty.
    (A) dog's bowls
    (B) dogs' bowls
    (C) dog's
    (D) dogs' bowl

15. The cat has a bed. _____ bed is comfortable.
    (A) It's
    (B) Its
    (C) Your
    (D) Their

**Find the *one* underlined word or phrase that must be changed for the sentence to be grammatically correct.**

16. Mickey <u>is</u> <u>a</u> famous <u>mice</u> at the <u>Florida</u> attraction Disney World.
        A  B          C              D

17. <u>That</u> is strange. <u>That man</u> <u>has</u> <u>three watchs</u> on his wrist.
      A              B      C        D

18. <u>That house</u> <u>have</u> heat in all of <u>the</u> rooms except <u>the</u> garage.
      A          B              C              D

19. <u>How many</u> does <u>a hamburger</u> cost at <u>that</u> new restaurant in <u>Orlando</u>?
      A              B              C                          D

20. <u>I have</u> a daughter. <u>My</u> <u>daughter's hair</u> is black like <u>my</u>.
      A              B      C                      D

21. <u>That</u> food is too spicy. <u>Her</u> has to drink <u>some water</u> with <u>her dinner</u>.
      A                    B              C              D

22. <u>Who</u> paper is <u>this</u>? It has <u>Joan's name</u> on it. I think it is <u>hers</u>.
      A          B          C                              D

23. Ludmilla <u>doesn't have</u> a book. Please give that book to <u>she</u>. <u>It</u> <u>is</u> <u>hers</u>.
                A                              B    C   D

**24.** <u>Whose</u> <u>homeworks are</u> on the table? I think <u>it's Sancho's</u> homework. He <u>doesn't have his</u>.
      A       B                                  C                D

**25.** <u>Do you have</u> <u>any biographies</u>? Yes, we have many books about <u>the lifes</u> of famous <u>people</u>.
      A               B                            C           D

# UNIT
# 7 There is/There are
## A/An versus The

**EXERCISE 1**   (Focus 1)

Look at the picture of Farmer Dell's farm. Underline the sentence in each pair that best describes this picture.

EXAMPLE:   A farm is in this picture.          <u>There is a farm in this picture</u>.

| | |
|---|---|
| **1.** There is a pig. | A pig is in the picture. |
| **2.** A horse is in the barn. | There is a horse in the barn. |
| **3.** Chickens are in the chicken coop. | There are chickens in the coop. |
| **4.** There is hay in the barn. | Hay is in the barn. |
| **5.** The goat is beside the barn. | There's a goat beside the barn. |
| **6.** The farmer is in his truck. | There's a farmer in the truck. |
| **7.** There are ducks on the pond. | Ducks are on the pond. |
| **8.** There is a rooster on the chicken coop. | A rooster is on the chicken coop. |
| **9.** There is corn in the field. | Some corn is in the field. |
| **10.** Two cows are in the barn. | There are two cows in the barn. |

There is/There are    **49**

Farmer McDonald has some problems on his farm. There are twelve things wrong with this picture. Write affirmative statements about the picture with *There + be* using the cues given.

EXAMPLE:  horse  <u>There is a horse on the roof.</u>

**1.** pig _____

**2.** chickens _____

**3.** corn _____

**4.** goat, duck, rooster _____

**5.** TV _____

**6.** electricity _____

**7.** cows _____

**8.** hat _____

**9.** glasses _____

**10.** dog _____

**11.** furniture _____

Cecilia is choosing a college. She likes the academic program and teachers at New College, but she wants to have more services and facilities. Cecilia made a list of things she would like New College to have. Change the list into negative statements using *There + be*.

EXAMPLE:    smoking area in the classroom  *There's no smoking area in the classroom.*

1. swimming pool _____

_____

2. job counselors _____

_____

3. college radio station _____

_____

4. public transportation into town _____

_____

5. cultural events _____

_____

6. golf course _____

_____

7. math tutor _____

_____

8. drugstore close to campus _____

_____

9. quiet places to study _____

_____

10. soccer team _____

_____

Imagine that you are trying to choose a school or college. Using the cues, write questions about the services and facilities available at the school.

EXAMPLE:    job counselors  *Are there any job counselors?*

1. academic counselors_____

_____

**2.** library _____

_____

**3.** scholarships _____

_____

**4.** financial aid money _____

_____

**5.** sports teams _____

_____

**6.** bookstore _____

_____

**7.** student clubs _____

_____

**8.** tutors _____

_____

**9.** dorms _____

_____

**10.** entertainment _____

_____

**EXERCISE 5**   (*Focus 5*)

Choose the definite or the indefinite article (*a, an,* or *the*) for each blank. The first one has been done for you as an example.

### A Friend's Birthday

Cristina went to ___*a*___ bakery to buy a cake. _____ bakery is new—it just opened last month. _____ cake is for _____ friend's birthday.

_____ friend's name is Lola. She is from Colombia. This is _____ first birthday Lola is celebrating without her family. Cristina doesn't want Lola to feel bad because she isn't with her family.

Cristina wants to buy Lola _____ special present. But _____ present can't cost too much because Cristina doesn't have much money. Cristina is looking for _____ umbrella. She thinks that _____ umbrella will make _____ practical and beautiful gift.

When she finds _____ perfect umbrella she tries to wrap it in colorful paper, but _____ umbrella is _____ difficult present to wrap. Finally, Cristina just puts _____ big bow on _____ umbrella.

When Cristina gives Lola _____ present and _____ cake Lola is surprised. She is happy to have _____ good friend like Cristina.

# UNIT 8

# Simple Present Tense

## Affirmative and Negative Statements, Time Expressions: *In/On/At*, *Like/Need/Want*

---

**EXERCISE 1** (*Focus 1*)

Read the stories about Thad and Cara and then underline each of the present tense verbs.

Thad Thrifty always tries to save money and resources. Before he goes grocery shopping he checks the advertisements in the newspaper and cuts out coupons to save money. He uses cold water to wash his clothes to save energy, and dries them outside on a clothesline when the weather is nice. He conserves electricity whenever possible. For example, he always turns off lights when he leaves a room.

Cara Careless spends money all the time. She buys food because it looks tasty. She forgets to plan meals so she eats out a lot. She wastes water when she washes her car. She always forgets to turn off her stereo when she leaves the house. She always dries her clothes in the dryer, even in warm weather.

**Choose the correct word given in parentheses to complete the story. Be sure the subject and the verb agree. The first one has been done for you as an example.**

I _____ **want** _____ (want, wants) you to meet my friend Herb Ban and his wife, Sunny. They _____ (live, lives) in the city. Herb _____ (like, likes) the city because his apartment is close to his job. Herb _____ (walk, walks) to work every morning. He _____ (work, works) in the building across the street from his apartment.

In the winter, Herb _____ (go, goes) to work without getting cold. He just _____ (walk, walks) through a tunnel that _____ (go, goes) between the two buildings.

Sunny, Herb's wife, _____ (think, thinks) the city is all right, but she _____ (prefer, prefers) the country. Sunny _____ (enjoy, enjoys) camping in the mountains. Every summer, they _____ (camp, camps) in Montana for two weeks. Herb always _____ (complain, complains) about the mosquitoes. He _____ (hate, hates) mosquitoes.

Personally, I _____ (want, wants) to live in the country, but I'm like Herb. I _____ (work, works) in the city.

**Do you try to save money and energy? Check the statements below that are generally true for you. Then compare your answers with a partner. Write true statements about your and your partner's habits.**

EXAMPLES: *I save coupons.*

*Sam reads the labels carefully before he buys something.*

*We both check advertisements for sales on food or clothing.*

1. _____ I check advertisements for sales on food or clothes.

2. _____ I save coupons.

3. _____ I read labels carefully before I buy something.

4. _____ I plan my meals.

5. _____ I conserve water.

6. _____ I wash my clothes in cold water.

7. _____ I dry my clothes on a clothesline.

8. _____ I eat at restaurants most of the time.

9. _____ I waste water when I brush my teeth.

10. _____ I forget to turn off lights when I leave the room.

11. _____ I always dry my clothes in a dryer.


## EXERCISE 4    (Focus 3)

Write statements about a family member using ten of the verbs below. Read the statements to your partner. Try to say each verb correctly in the third person. If possible, record yourself on tape and listen to your pronunciation.

| make | clean | wash | work | iron | rush | walk |
| fight | run | fix | sleep | swim | mix | read |
| watch | help | freeze | eat | like | wish | cook |

EXAMPLE:    _My brother fights with my little sister._

1. _____

2. _____

3. _____

4. _____

5. _____

6. _____

7. _____

8. _____

9. _____

10. _____

Finish the story with the correct form of each verb given in parentheses. Be careful of spelling. Then read the story out loud. If possible, record yourself and listen for the correct pronunciation of the verbs. The first one has been done for you as an example.

Norman _____goes_____ (go) to work on the bus. He _____ (hurry) to the bus stop because he doesn't want to miss the bus. Norman _____ (enjoy) his work, but he _____ (worry) when he is late. His boss _____ (have) strict rules about being on time.

Norman _____ (work) for a toy company. He _____ (test) toys. Every morning Norman _____ (have) a box of new toys on his desk. First he _____ (empty) the box and _____ (look) at the toys he will test. Then Norman _____ (play) with the toys. He (try) them out.

After he _____ (see) what a toy _____ (do), Norman _____ (write) a report about the toy. The report _____ (say) what age child the toy is best for. It also _____ (tell) about any possible dangers to children. Then Norman _____ (send) his report and the toy to his boss.

**EXERCISE 6** (*Focus 4*)

Using the cues, make two true statements about yourself by adding a time expression or a frequency expression. Skip the statements that are not true for you.

EXAMPLE:  go to school _____I go to school three days a week._____
_____I go to school in the morning._____

1. go to school _____
_____

2. eat pizza _____
_____

3. see your family_____
_____

4. drink water _____
_____

5. call your mother _____
_____

6. cook a meal _____
_____

7. watch TV _____

_____

8. go to the dentist _____

_____

9. eat Chinese food _____

_____

10. wash your clothes _____

_____

11. pay your bills _____

_____

12. read the newspaper _____

_____

## EXERCISE 7 (*Focus 5*)

Make a list of things that you usually do in each of the following time periods. Then write sentences about your activities using *in*, *at*, *on*, or *no preposition*.

EXAMPLES: summer

take a vacation  In the summer I usually take a vacation.

go camping  I usually go camping in the summer.

**summer**

1. _____
2. _____
3. _____

**Monday**

1. _____
2. _____
3. _____

**noon**

1. _____
2. _____
3. _____

**weekends**

1. _____

2. _____

3. _____

**December**

1. _____

2. _____

3. _____

**EXERCISE 8** (*Focus 5*)

**Ask your partner the following questions, using the information in Exercise 7 to help with the answers.**

EXAMPLE:   **A:** What do you usually do in the summer?

**B:** I *usually take a vacation. I usually go camping in the summer.*

1. What do you usually do in the summer?

2. What do you usually do on Mondays?

3. What do you usually do at noon?

4. What do you usually do on weekends?

5. What do you usually do in December?

Don and Ron are brothers. They are different in some ways and the same in others. Look at the information about Don and Ron and, using the cues given, make negative sentences.

**DON**

Don is an accountant; he works in a big office downtown. He has a sports car and lives in an apartment. Still, Don likes to stay healthy. He likes exercise, but he doesn't like jogging. He enjoys playing basketball with his friends. He likes to do active things. He doesn't like going to the movies. He is a vegetarian, and he doesn't smoke.

**RON**

Ron is a park ranger; he works outdoors. He has a pick-up truck and lives in a house. Ron likes to stay healthy. He likes exercise, but he doesn't like jogging. He prefers playing volleyball with his friends. Ron doesn't like basketball or movies. He doesn't smoke, and he is a vegetarian.

EXAMPLES:    *Don doesn't work outside.*

*Don and Ron don't eat meat.*

**1.** work inside _____

_____

**2.** live in a house _____

_____

**3.** smoke _____

_____

**4.** have a sports car _____

_____

**5.** play volleyball _____

_____

**6.** jog _____

_____

**7.** like team sports _____

_____

**8.** drive a pick-up truck _____

_____

**9.** live in an apartment _____

_____

**10.** like movies _____

_____

**11.** like basketball _____

_____


## EXERCISE 10 (Focus 7)

**Read the list of activities below and ask yourself if good parents do each of them. Choose yes or no and then complete each statement making it affirmative or negative.**

|  | YES | NO |
|---|---|---|
| EXAMPLE: let their children stay up late every night | _____ | __X__ |

*Good parents don't let their children stay up late every night.*

| | YES | NO |
|---|---|---|
| **1.** play in the street | _____ | _____ |
| **2.** make their children do chores | _____ | _____ |
| **3.** give their children an allowance (weekly money) | _____ | _____ |
| **4.** let their children watch TV five hours every day | _____ | _____ |
| **5.** leave their children at home alone | _____ | _____ |

|  | YES | NO |
|---|---|---|
| **6.** give their children cigarettes | _____ | _____ |
| **7.** feed their children healthy food | _____ | _____ |
| **8.** help their children with their homework | _____ | _____ |
| **9.** let their children go to the library | _____ | _____ |
| **10.** buy their children bicycles | _____ | _____ |

## EXERCISE 11 (*Focus 8*)

You and your partner are going to take a trip to Europe together. Make a list of all the things you plan to take with you and the places you plan to see. Then, for each item on your list, decide if you want, like, or need to take it or see it. Then share your vacation plans with another group.

EXAMPLE:

| THINGS | TO DO |
|---|---|
| **Write:** | |
| sweaters—need | see Paris |
| camera—want | take photos |
| **Then tell another pair:** | |
| We need sweaters. | We need to see Paris. |
| We want a camera. | We want to take photos. |

| THINGS | TO DO |
|---|---|
| 1. | 1. |
| 2. | 2. |
| 3. | 3. |
| 4. | 4. |
| 5. | 5. |
| 6. | 6. |
| 7. | 7. |
| 8. | 8. |

# UNIT 9
# Simple Present Tense

## Yes/No Questions, Adverbs of Frequency, Wh-Questions

**EXERCISE 1**   (*Focus 1*)

**Using the cues, write yes/no questions. Then ask your partner the questions. Record his or her short answers.**

EXAMPLE:   watch sports on TV  _Do you watch sports on TV?_

   _Yes, I do._ or _No, I don't._

1. watch sports on TV _____

   _____

2. sing in the shower _____

   _____

3. work _____

   _____

4. have a hobby _____

   _____

5. believe in ghosts _____

   _____

6. cook your own meals _____

   _____

7. like to dance _____

   _____

8. take vacations _____

   _____

9. have a pet _____

   _____

10. play chess _____

   _____

Change partners. Ask your new partner about his or her first partner using the cues from Exercise 1. Record his or her short answers.

EXAMPLE:   watch sports on TV___*Does Mohamad watch sports on TV?*___

*Yes, he does.*___

1. watch sports on TV _____

_____

2. sing in the shower _____

_____

3. work _____

_____

4. have a hobby _____

_____

5. believe in ghosts _____

_____

6. cook his/her own meals _____

_____

7. like to dance _____

_____

8. take vacations _____

_____

9. have a pet _____

_____

10. play chess _____

_____

## EXERCISE 3 (Focus 2)

The list below shows healthy and unhealthy habits and adverbs of frequency. Check the box for each that is true for you.

### Adverbs of Frequency

| Habits | Always | Almost always | Usually | Often; Frequently | Sometimes | Seldom; Rarely | Never |
|---|---|---|---|---|---|---|---|
| 1. exercise | | | | | | | |
| 2. eat fresh vegetables | | | | | | | |
| 3. sleep eight hours | | | | | | | |
| 4. relax | | | | | | | |
| 5. drink water | | | | | | | |
| 6. take vitamins | | | | | | | |
| 7. eat junk food | | | | | | | |
| 8. drink alcohol | | | | | | | |
| 9. drive too fast | | | | | | | |
| 10. smoke cigarettes | | | | | | | |
| 11. get sunburned | | | | | | | |

## EXERCISE 4 (Focus 3)

Using your answers from Exercise 3, write sentences about your healthy and unhealthy habits. Compare your answers with your classmates.

EXAMPLE:  I frequently exercise.

1. _____

2. _____

3. _____

4. _____

5. _____

6. _____

7. _____

8. _____

9. _____

10. _____

11. _____


## EXERCISE 5 (Focus 4)

**Fanny Fad, a reporter for *Teen Star* magazine, interviewed these teenage stars. Read each article and then finish the questions Fanny asked, using the cues. The first one has been done for you as an example.**

### Chris Crash, 15

Chris Crash likes to skateboard. He likes skateboarding because it is a fast sport. Chris lives in California. He practices skateboarding every day after school. He learns new skateboard tricks by studying other skateboarders. Chris wants to act in a skateboard movie.

1. What ___*do you like to do?*___

2. Why _____

3. Where _____

4. How often _____

5. When _____

6. How _____

7. What _____

**Suzy Flex, 13**

Suzy likes gymnastics. She practices hard because she wants to compete in the summer Olympics. She rehearses her gymnastic routines twice a day at the gym. She practices at 5:00 every morning and 4:30 every afternoon. She learns new routines with the help of her coach.

1. What _____

2. Why _____

3. How often _____

4. Where _____

5. What time _____

6. How _____

7. When _____

## EXERCISE 6   (*Focus 4*)

**Write the question that goes with each of the answers. Use the underlined words as cues.**

EXAMPLE:   *Where does your mother live?* _____

My mother lives <u>in Brazil</u>.

1. _____

I call my parents <u>once a week</u> on Saturday.

2. _____

My parents <u>wait</u> for my call.

3. _____

They wait <u>because they know I will always call on time</u>.

4. _____

I call at <u>8 P.M</u>.

5. _____

My brother lives <u>in Brazil</u> also.

**6.** _____

He is a clerk in a government office.

**7.** _____

He works in Brasilia.

**8.** _____

My parents live in São Paulo.

**9.** _____

He lives in Brasilia because it is the capital of Brazil.

**10.** _____

My brother goes to São Paulo on holidays.

## EXERCISE 7 (Focus 5)

**Read the story. Write "who or whom" questions to go with each answer, using the underlined words as cues.**

Jill, Mandy, and Joy are roommates. They share an apartment near the college they are attending. They share the responsibilities for the apartment and they also do many things together.

Jill drives Mandy and Joy to school every day. Joy makes dinner on weekdays and Mandy makes dinner on weekends. Joy's responsibility is to take out the trash on Mondays. Mandy puts out the recycling on Wednesdays. Jill washes her car on Saturdays.

Usually their friends Sam, Roy, and George eat dinner with them on Saturdays. Mandy and Jill also play tennis together.

EXAMPLE: _Who are Mandy's roommates?_ _____

Jill and Joy are Mandy's roommates.

**1.** _____

Mandy and Jill share an apartment with Joy.

**2.** _____

Mandy, Jill, and Joy go to school.

**3.** _____

Jill drives the car.

**4.** _____

Mandy and Joy ride with Jill.

**5.** _____

Joy cooks dinner on Tuesday.

**6.** _____

Mandy prepares dinner on the weekends.

**7.** _____

Joy takes out the trash.

**8.** _____

Mandy puts out the recycling.

**9.** _____

Jill washes her own car.

**10.** _____

They meet Sam, George, and Roy on Saturday night.

**11.** _____

Mandy and Jill play tennis.

**12.** _____

Jill plays tennis with Mandy.

## EXERCISE 8 (Focus 5)

**Read the following questions. Write "I" in front of the question if it is informal. Write "F" in front of the question if it is formal.**

EXAMPLE: ____F____ With whom will you be attending the party?

**1.** _____ Who will you give the flowers to?

**2.** _____ Whom can I expect to meet at the party?

**3.** _____ Whom is this package for?

**4.** _____ Who has my new hairdryer?

**5.** _____ Who wants ice cream?

**6.** _____ Who studies on weekends?

**7.** _____ With whom do you play tennis?

**8.** _____ Who sings the duet with you?

Read each question. If it is correct write "C" in front of it. If it is incorrect write "I" in front of it and rewrite the question correctly.

EXAMPLE: ___I___ How you pronounce "toothache"?

*How do you pronounce "toothache"?*

1. _____ How do you spell "sincerely"?

_____

2. _____ How you say the opposite of "tired"?

_____

3. _____ How to pronounce "potato"?

_____

4. _____ What means "illogical"?

_____

5. _____ What the word "frantic" means?

_____

6. _____ How do you say the opposite of freedom?

_____

7. _____ How spell "Wednesday"?

_____

8. _____ How you pronounce your name?

_____

9. _____ What do means "ethical"?

_____

10. _____ How you say a little wet?

_____

Using the appropriate questions, ask your partner about the items listed below. If neither of you knows the correct answer, look it up in a bilingual dictionary. Follow the example.

| OPPOSITES | SPELLING | PRONUNCIATION |
|---|---|---|
| boring | your name | through |
| relaxed | the capital of the United States | Illinois |
| winter | the President's name | your name |

| MEANING | DESCRIPTION |
|---|---|
| neither | a thing that a baby drinks from |
| upset | the square thing you put into a computer |
| obligatory | a chair with no back, just legs |

EXAMPLE:    **Q:** *What is the opposite of boring?*

**A:** *Interesting.*

**Choose the *one* word or phrase that best completes each sentence.**

1. _____ live in Baltimore?
   (A) Do she          (C) Does they
   (B) Do you          (D) Do he

2. Carmela gets home _____ 5:00 and prepares dinner.
   (A) at              (C) on
   (B) in              (D) to

3. Do you _____ work on Saturday? Yes, I _____ work on Saturdays.
   (A) usually…always      (C) never…always
   (B) ever…seldom         (D) ever…always

4. _____ a good restaurant near my apartment.
   (A) There are       (C) There is
   (B) Is it           (D) This

5. _____ any mail for me today?
   (A) Is              (C) Are
   (B) Are there       (D) Is there

6. _____ the bookstore open on Saturday?
   (A) When does       (C) Who does
   (B) What time do    (D) What does

7. Forrest Bowlins is a banker. He _____ people's money.
   (A) manages         (C) have to
   (B) manage          (D) wants a

8. Sheldon _____ a nap after school.
   (A) take            (C) wanting
   (B) does            (D) takes

9. Once a week, _____ Fridays, Diane goes dancing.
   (A) in              (C) on
   (B) at              (D) the

10. I celebrate my birthday _____ May 19th.
    (A) on the             (C) the
    (B) in                (D) on

11. A healthy person _____ eat hamburgers every day.
    (A) don't            (C) no
    (B) doesn't          (D) any

12. Chieko _____ want to miss class.
    (A) no              (C) don't
    (B) not             (D) doesn't

13. Enriqueta and Jo _____ about their friend.
    (A) worried         (C) are worried
    (B) are worry       (D) worrying

14. Charlie is always tired. He _____ sleep very well at night.
    (A) no              (C) not
    (B) isn't            (D) doesn't

15. _____ do you get to school? _____.
    (A) How...I take by bus     (C) How...I take the bus
    (B) What...By bus         (D) What...I ride

**Identify the *one* underlined word or phrase that must be changed for the sentence to be grammatically correct.**

16. She <u>makes plans</u> for her vacation <u>on December</u>. She decides <u>to go to the mountains</u>,
         A                     B                          C
    even though she likes <u>to go the beach</u>.
                         D

17. <u>There</u> <u>aren't</u> <u>any milk</u> <u>in the refrigerator</u>.
    A      B      C         D

18. The <u>Italian restaurant</u> <u>is open</u>, but <u>it no have</u> <u>any linguine</u> today.
        A            B           C        D

19. <u>The sun</u> <u>rises always</u> in the east and <u>sets</u> <u>in the west</u>.
    A        B                 C    D

20. <u>Many</u> people <u>in India</u> <u>don't eats</u> meat; they <u>only eat</u> vegetables.
    A          B       C             D

21. <u>In the winter</u>, they <u>go for ski</u> <u>in the mountains</u> <u>in Colorado</u>.
    A              B         C        D

22. <u>Is there</u> anything for the children <u>to do</u> <u>in the summer</u>? They <u>go to swimming</u>.
    A                      B    C            D

**23.** <u>I need</u> <u>to do a phone call</u> before <u>we make a decision</u> about <u>the new car</u>.
       A                  B                            C                  D

**24.** Blanca <u>doesn't goes</u> <u>to the university</u> <u>on Fridays</u> <u>in December</u>.
                 A             B             C         D

**25.** <u>There is</u> a word <u>I don't know</u>. <u>What means</u> sibling? <u>It means</u> a brother or a sister.
       A                 B          C         D

# Imperatives and Prepositions of Direction

---

**EXERCISE 1**    (*Focus 1*)

Using the pictures and cues, write affirmative, negative, or polite imperative sentences.

EXAMPLE:   Affirmative: _Stay away!_ _____

               Negative: _Don't touch!_ _____

**1.**

Affirmative: _____

_____

Polite: _____

_____

**2.**

Affirmative: _____

_____

Polite: _____

_____

**3.**

Affirmative: _____

_____

Negative: _____

_____

**4.**

Affirmative: _____

_____

Polite: _____

_____

**5.**

Affirmative: _____

_____

Polite: _____

_____

**6.**

Affirmative: _____

_____

Negative: _____

_____

**7.**

Affirmative: _____

_____

Polite: _____

_____

**8.**

Affirmative: _____

_____

Negative: _____

_____

**Study each of the following examples and write the function of each imperative next to the example.**

## FUNCTIONS

- Giving advice
- Giving an order
- Giving a warning when there is danger
- Making a polite request
- Politely offering something
- Giving directions

EXAMPLE:    Do not expose to heat. Keep out of the reach of children. Avoid freezing.

*Giving a warning when there is danger*

1. Mix the butter and the sugar well. Beat in the molasses. Add the flour, soda, cloves, cinnamon, ginger, and salt.

2. Danger: Harmful if swallowed. Read caution on back label carefully.

3. Bring me that report.

4. Please, eat some more pot roast.

5. Please gift wrap this.

6. Remember to call if you have a problem. Eat well and get enough sleep.

## EXERCISE 3 (Focus 3)

Check "yes" if the imperative is appropriate in the situation. Check "no" if it is not appropriate. Check "depends" if you think it could be appropriate in certain situations.

| Situation | Imperative | Yes | No | Depends |
|---|---|---|---|---|
| EXAMPLE:<br>Son to father: | Give me the car keys! | | × | |
| 1. Police officer to teenager: | Don't drive so fast! | | | |
| 2. Student to teacher: | Tell me the answer. | | | |
| 3. Patient to doctor: | Please, fill out these insurance forms. | | | |
| 4. Lawyer to client: | Don't say anything to the police. | | | |
| 5. Employee to boss: | Give me the report! | | | |
| 6. Dentist to patient: | Brush your teeth three times a day. | | | |
| 7. Roommate to roommate: | Please answer the phone. | | | |

## EXERCISE 4 (Focus 3)

For each inappropriate imperative from Exercise 3, rewrite the imperative in the appropriate form.

EXAMPLE: _Dad, please give me the car keys._

_____

_____

_____

_____

_____

**Read the following sentences. For each, if the sentence is correct, write "C" in front of it. If the sentence is incorrect, write "I" in front of it and rewrite the sentence to make it correct.**

EXAMPLE: ___I___ Debbie lives off 1638 Perma Drive.

*Debbie lives at 1638 Perma Drive.* _____

1. _____ She works at 400 State Street. _____

_____

2. _____ Debbie's office is out of the seventh floor. _____

_____

3. _____ Every morning she is late for work, so Debbie runs on her house. _____

_____

4. _____ She drives out of her driveway. _____

_____

5. _____ She turns left out of her neighborhood and gets on the freeway. _____

_____

6. _____ Debbie gets at the freeway when she gets downtown. _____

_____

7. _____ She rushes out of her car and goes to the elevator. _____

_____

8. _____ She runs at the elevator. _____

_____

9. _____ She gets off on the seventh floor just in time. _____

_____

10. _____ When her boss arrives, Debbie is off her desk. _____

_____

You need three people to do this activity. The first person whispers the directions below to the second person. The second person must follow the directions. The third person writes down what she or he sees the second person do. You should begin outside of your classroom.

EXAMPLE:    Whisper: *Walk into the class.*

Write: *Joseph walks into the class.*

1. Walk into the classroom.

2. Run to the desk.

3. Put your book on the desk.

4. Tiptoe away from the desk.

5. Walk back to the desk.

6. Take your book off of the desk.

7. Jump out of the classroom.

**Change roles. The first person can change the order of the activities.**

**Match the sentence with the activity in the picture.**

1. The boy walks through the mud.
2. The girl slides down the slide.
3. The joggers run along the path.
4. The girl walks around the mud.
5. The children walk across the balance beam.
6. The children climb up the ladder.
7. The woman runs past the man.
8. The old man walks over the bridge.
9. The boy crawls through the tunnel.
10. The girl swings across the bars.
11. The boy climbs up the bars.

# UNIT

# 11 Quantifiers

**EXERCISE 1** *(Focus 1)*

Look at the picture of the five food groups. Decide which foods are count and which are noncount nouns. Write the name of each food in the proper category.

MEATS

MILK & DAIRY

MILK

YOGURT

SHORTENING    OIL

FATS & OILS

CEREAL

FLOUR

RICE

BREADS & CEREALS

DUANE GILLOGLY

FRUITS & VEGETABLES

| COUNT | NONCOUNT |
|-------|----------|
|       |          |
|       |          |
|       |          |
|       |          |
|       |          |
|       |          |
|       |          |
|       |          |
|       |          |
|       |          |

Look at what Wendy Weightlifter and Skinny Sarah had for breakfast and lunch, and then complete the sentences below using *many, a lot of, some, a few, a little, few, any, no, much, very little,* or *any.* There is more than one correct answer for some of the blanks. Compare your answers with a classmate. The first one has been done for you.

**WENDY WEIGHTLIFTER**

| Breakfast | Lunch |
|---|---|
| four eggs | chicken |
| orange juice | onion rings |
| bacon | four apples |
| three pieces of toast | three sodas |

**SKINNY SARAH**

| Breakfast | Lunch |
|---|---|
| yogurt | vegetable soup |
| cup of coffee | milk |
| bagel | salad |
| | grapes |

Wendy had **(1)** _____some_____ eggs for breakfast. She also drank **(2)** _____ orange juice. She ate **(3)** _____ bacon. Finally, she ate **(4)** _____ toast.

Sarah didn't eat **(5)** _____ for breakfast. She had **(6)** _____ yogurt. She drank **(7)** _____ coffee and ate a bagel with **(8)** _____ jam.

Wendy also had a big lunch. She ate **(9)** _____ of chicken, **(10)** _____ onion rings, and **(11)** _____ apples. She also drank **(12)** _____ soda.

Sarah didn't have **(13)** _____ chicken for lunch. She had **(14)** _____ soup, **(15)** _____ salad, and **(16)** _____ grapes. She drank **(17)** _____ milk.

## EXERCISE 3  (Focus 2)

Write three sentences about what you ate yesterday using the quantifiers in the directions from Exercise 2.

_____

_____

_____

## EXERCISE 4  (Focus 3)

Wendy is training for a bodybuilding competition. She needs to lose some weight before the competition, and she decided the best way to lose it would be to go to training camp. However, Wendy is not very happy at camp. Finish the letter she wrote to her mother with *a few, a little, few* or *little.* The first one has been done for you.

Dear Mom,

I hope everything is ok at home. I'm having _____*a few*_____ problems here at fat camp. I'm glad that I only have **(1)** _____ more time here. I'm ready to go home.

First, I wish we could have **(2)** _____ more food. There is so **(3)** _____ food at breakfast that I'm starving by 10:00. All I had for breakfast were **(4)** _____ grapes, **(5)** _____ milk, and a piece of toast with **(6)** _____ margarine.

Another problem is the exercise program. We are always doing something: lifting weights, walking, swimming, or riding bikes. We have **(7)** _____ time to relax. At the end of the day I have **(8)** _____ energy. I can barely make it into bed. Then we have so **(9)** _____ hours to sleep. They wake us up at 6:00 and we go to bed at 10:00. I am exhausted.

The only good thing is that I've made **(10)** _____ friends. There are three girls in my cabin who are also trying to lose **(11)** _____ weight for the competition.

I will be home in three days. Thank goodness I only have **(12)** _____ more time here. Maybe I can lose **(13)** _____ weight in **(14)** _____ more days on this diet.

Your daughter,
Wendy

## EXERCISE 5 (Focus 4)

**Write the questions about what Wendy and Sarah ate using How much or How many. Refer to Exercise 2 if you need to.**

EXAMPLE: *How many onion rings did she eat?*
She ate twelve onion rings.

1. _____

She drank one cup of coffee for breakfast.

2. _____

She didn't have any hot dogs for lunch.

3. _____

Wendy drank a lot of orange juice for breakfast.

4. _____

She didn't eat much for breakfast. She ate just a little.

5. _____

She had a little vegetable soup.

6. _____

She ate four apples for lunch.

7. _____

She didn't eat any grapes for lunch.

8. _____

Sarah didn't have any soup for lunch.

9. _____

Sarah ate a lot of yogurt for breakfast.

10. _____

She had a little milk at lunch.


## EXERCISE 6 (Focus 5)

**Wendy is home from training camp and wants to go grocery shopping, so her mother told her to make a shopping list. Look at the things Wendy is thinking of buying and write Wendy's list using the correct measure word. The first one has been done for you as an example.**

1. _a loaf of bread_
2. _____
3. _____

4. _____

5. _____

6. _____

7. _____

8. _____

9. _____

10. _____

11. _____

12. _____

# UNIT

# Adverbs of Manner

**EXERCISE 1**   (*Focus 1*)

**Take turns with your partner asking the following questions. Answer using complete sentences. Write each other's answers.**

EXAMPLE:   **A:** Are you calm or nervous when you take tests?

**B:**   *I'm calm when I take a test.*

1. Are you calm or nervous when you take tests? _____

_____

2. Are you calm or nervous when you take tests? _____

_____

3. Are you grumpy or cheerful when you wake up in the morning? _____

_____

4. Are your clothes loose or tight? _____

_____

5. Are you a heavy or a light exerciser? _____

_____

6. Are you shy or outgoing when you meet a new person? _____

_____

7. Are you slow or quick when you walk somewhere? _____

_____

8. Are you careful or careless when you drive? _____

_____

*Adverbs of Manner*      **87**

**Write answers to the following questions about your partner using complete sentences.**

EXAMPLE:    Does your partner take tests calmly?

_Yes, she (or he) takes tests calmly._

1. Does your partner take tests calmly? _____

   _____

2. Does your partner wake up grumpily? _____

   _____

3. Do your partner's clothes fit loosely? _____

   _____

4. Does your partner exercise heavily? _____

   _____

5. Does your partner meet new people easily? _____

   _____

6. Does your partner walk quickly? _____

   _____

7. Does your partner drive carelessly? _____

   _____

**Using the information from this story, fill in the blanks in the second story using adverbs instead of adjectives. The first one has been done for you.**

Mom was early coming home, because her shopping trip was terrible. She was enthusiastic when she left the house because there were many new clothes she wanted to buy.

First she tried on a blue skirt. The skirt looked good, but the fit wasn't terrific. It was loose. So she tried on a black skirt, but it was tight. When she took the skirt off she was careless, and the zipper broke. She tried to be careful when she fixed the zipper, but it got stuck. She couldn't get the skirt on or off. She became anxious and pulled on the zipper, but it still wouldn't move. She didn't know what to do. Even though she felt shy, she called for a saleswoman. The saleswoman was glad to help. She tried to unzip the skirt, but she was also unsuccessful. Mom was brave. She was calm as she waited. The saleswoman got some scissors and made a neat cut near the zipper. Mom was quick to leave the store.

Mom came home ____*early*____ because her shopping trip went _____. She left _____ because there were many new clothes she wanted to buy.

First she tried on a blue skirt. The skirt looked like it would fit _____, but it didn't fit _____. It fit _____. So she tried on a black skirt but it fit _____. She took the skirt off _____ and the zipper broke. She tried to fix the zipper _____, but it got stuck. She couldn't get the skirt on or off. She pulled _____ on the zipper, but it still wouldn't move. She didn't know what to do. She called for a saleswoman _____. The saleswoman _____ helped. She _____ tried to unzip the skirt. Mom stood _____ and waited _____. The saleswoman got some scissors and cut _____ near the zipper. Mom left the store _____.

What do you know about the different jobs below? Using the cues, write two sentences for each job. One sentence focuses on the person; the other sentence focuses on the person's action.

EXAMPLE:    Receptionist/polite

**person:**    *A receptionist is polite on the phone.*

**action:**    *A receptionist answers the phone politely.*

1. Model/attractive

**person:** _____

**action:** _____

2. Waitress/quick

**person:** _____

**action:** _____

3. Nurse/calm

**person:** _____

**action:** _____

4. Truck driver/careful

**person:** _____

**action:** _____

5. Mechanic/messy

**person:** _____

**action:** _____

6. Race car driver/fast

**person:** _____

**action:** _____

7. Scientist/systematic

**person:** _____

**action:** _____

8. Pilot/cautious

**person:** _____

**action:** _____

**9.** Construction worker/noisy

**person:** _____

**action:** _____

**10.** The president/diplomatic

**person:** _____

**action:** _____

**EXERCISE 5**　　(*Focus 3*)

**Think of a person, place, action, or thing that fits each category below. Write a sentence using the intensifier *very*.**

EXAMPLE:　a car that goes fast

_____*A Corvette goes very fast.*_____

**1.** a basketball player who jumps high

_____

**2.** an athlete who runs well

_____

**3.** someone in your class who reads quickly

_____

**4.** a person who works sloppily

_____

**5.** someone who sings beautifully

_____

**6.** a plant that grows slowly

_____

**7.** someone in your class who shops carefully

_____

**8.** an actress who speaks softly

_____

**9.** a restaurant where you can buy good food cheaply

_____

**10.** a writer who writes poetically

_____

**11.** an animal that runs quickly

_____

Make a group of four students. Compare your answers from Exercise 5 with other group members' answers. Choose the best answer for each category. Share those answers with the rest of the students in your class.

# TOEFL®

# Test Preparation Exercises
## Units 10–12

**Choose the *one* word or phrase that best completes each sentence.**

1. Kim likes ice cream, but _____ makes her cold.
   - (A) she
   - (B) it
   - (C) he
   - (D) you

2. Artie and Gilberto go _____ Los Angeles every year.
   - (A) in
   - (B) on
   - (C) to
   - (D) at

3. Monica rushes _____ work every Friday afternoon.
   - (A) quickly out of
   - (B) quick out of
   - (C) quick out at
   - (D) quickly out at

4. I need _____ minutes to find my keys.
   - (A) little
   - (B) a little
   - (C) few
   - (D) a few

5. The teacher walked _____ the classroom.
   - (A) fastly through
   - (B) through quietly
   - (C) quietly through
   - (D) through fastly

6. Drink _____ water instead of _____ cola.
   - (A) some glass of…one
   - (B) a glass of…a bottle of
   - (C) a can of…a glass of
   - (D) a…a bottle of

7. Betty is very careful with her money; she save money _____.
   - (A) careful
   - (B) carefully
   - (C) careless
   - (D) carelessly

8. At the grocery store Alice buys _____.
   - (A) a dozen of eggs
   - (B) a pound of orange
   - (C) a cup of grapes
   - (D) a head of lettuce

9. _____! That car is out of control!
   - (A) Watch out
   - (B) Please turn right
   - (C) Put on your blinker when you turn
   - (D) Please, try my new car

10. The marathon race goes _____ the center of the city and _____ the bridge.
    (A) through…up
    (B) past…through
    (C) through…across
    (D) over…down

11. The rice is always overcooked. Please, _____.
    (A) watch it carefully
    (B) it watch carefully
    (C) you watch it careful
    (D) watch you it careful

12. A tornado can blow a roof _____ a house.
    (A) out of
    (B) off of
    (C) at
    (D) down

13. _____ First Street.
    (A) Turn left on
    (B) You turn
    (C) Turn left into
    (D) Turn you on

14. There are many fast-food restaurants _____ the highway.
    (A) to
    (B) along
    (C) into
    (D) out of

15. When the cat and dog need food I give _____ some.
    (A) it
    (B) they
    (C) them
    (D) him


**Identify the *one* underlined word or phrase that must be changed for the sentence to be grammatically correct.**


16. <u>Enrique has</u> many new books; <u>he reads</u> <u>quick</u> <u>during the winter break</u>.
    　　A　　　　　　　　　　　　B　　C　　　　D

17. <u>I need</u> <u>to buy</u> <u>a little</u> things <u>at the store</u>.
    　A　　B　　　C　　　　　　　D

18. Excuse me, <u>how do I get to the park</u>? <u>Go straight</u>. <u>Walk one block</u>. Then <u>turn in the corner</u>
    　　　　　　　A　　　　　　　　　　B　　　　　C　　　　　　　　D
    of Central Avenue.

19. Please <u>has</u> <u>a little</u> more juice. Thanks, it's delicious. <u>Where</u> did you buy it? <u>At the fruit stand</u>.
    　　　　A　　B　　　　　　　　　　　　　　　　　　C　　　　　　　　　D

20. <u>How do I get there</u>? <u>Walk</u> <u>at the corner</u> and <u>turn left</u>.
    　　A　　　　　　　　B　　C　　　　　　D

21. <u>There are</u> <u>few apples</u> <u>in the refrigerator</u>. Please <u>bring me one</u>.
    　　A　　　　B　　　　　C　　　　　　　　　　D

22. After <u>they climb</u> <u>up</u> the mountain, the <u>explorers climb</u> <u>off of</u> the mountain.
    　　　A　　　　B　　　　　　　　　　C　　　　　D

**23.** <u>How much is</u> <u>a box of cereal</u>? <u>I'm not sure</u>. Please <u>to check price</u>.
      A           B           C                D

**24.** The helicopter always flies <u>up the city</u>. <u>The pilot looks</u> for traffic accidents. He tells the
                                   A            B

drivers <u>on the ground</u> how to get <u>away from traffic jams</u>.
         C                        D

# UNIT

# 13 Direct and Indirect Objects, Direct and Indirect Pronouns

**EXERCISE 1** **(Focus 1)**

  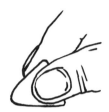

**Underline the direct object in each sentence.**

EXAMPLE:   Many people play <u>guitars</u>.

1. Other people enjoy guitar music.

2. The guitar has six strings.

3. Each string plays a different note.

4. Guitarists change the notes.

5. They push each string against the neck of the guitar with the fingers of the left hand.

6. This makes the string shorter.

7. The shorter string produces a higher note.

8. Guitarists usually strum the guitar with their right hand.

9. Sometimes they use a pick to pluck the strings.

10. Americans use guitars for many types of music.

11. Acoustic guitars accompany folk music.

12. Rock musicians use electric guitars.

**Choose the correct pronouns to complete the story. The first one has been done for you as an example.**

Today starts off bad. My dad wakes up late. __He__ (He, Him) is in a bad mood and _____ (he, him) gets a cut while _____ (he, him) is shaving. _____ (He, Him) is grumpy. When my mom gives _____ (he, him) breakfast, _____ (he, him) gets mad at _____ (she, her) This makes my mom angry. _____ (She, Her) yells at my big brother. _____ (She, her) gets mad at _____ (he, him) for no reason. My brother shouts at _____ (I, me). _____ (I, me) feel bad. _____ (I, me) yell at Ruff, my dog. Ruff just looks at _____ (I, me). Ruff barks at _____ (I, me) and gives _____ (I, me) a big kiss. The kiss tickles _____ (I, me).

**Read the paragraph, noticing the underlined object pronouns. Draw an arrow from each object pronoun to the noun phrase it refers to and circle the noun phrase. The first one has been done for you as an example.**

I don't feel mad at (my family) any more. I want <u>them</u> to feel happy. I have to do something for <u>them</u>. I go outside and pick some beautiful flowers. I give <u>them</u> to my brother, mother, and father. My brother smiles at <u>me</u>. My mother gives <u>me</u> a kiss. I give <u>her</u> a hug. My father smiles at me too. I give <u>him</u> a hug also. My family is laughing. I really like <u>them</u> when they are happy. Ruff is happy too; my brother is petting <u>him</u>. Ruff finds some milk on the floor and licks <u>it</u> up. When you are happy, everyone is happy with <u>you</u>.

**Read the story. For each sentence, write the direct object in the first column and the indirect object that follows in the second column. The first one has been done for you (not all sentences have indirect objects).**

## Birthday Surprise

EXAMPLE: Josh plays music for his friends.

1. He sings special songs for his friends.
2. They plan a surprise party for Josh.
3. Gwen makes a cake for Josh.
4. Ben buys the decorations for the party.
5. They want to buy a special present for him.
6. His friends put their money together for a new guitar.
7. They all give some money to Len.
8. At the music store Len finds the perfect guitar for Josh.
9. Len gives the gift to Josh.
10. Josh loves the new guitar.
11. Josh sings a special song to his friends.

| DIRECT OBJECT | INDIRECT OBJECT |
|---|---|
| example: music | friends |
| 1. | |
| 2. | |
| 3. | |
| 4. | |
| 5. | |
| 6. | |
| 7. | |
| 8. | |
| 9. | |
| 10. | |
| 11. | |

**Rewrite the sentences by putting the indirect object before the direct object.**

EXAMPLE:    They plan to give a surprise party for Josh.

*They plan to give Josh a surprise party.*

1. Gwen makes a cake for Josh. _____

_____

2. They all give some money to Len. _____

_____

3. The man hands the new guitar to Len. _____

_____

4. Len gives the guitar to Josh. _____

_____

5. Josh gives his old guitar to Gwen. _____

_____

6. On the weekends, Josh gives guitar lessons to the children in his building. _____

_____

7. He teaches music to the children. _____

_____

8. He also finds used guitars for the children. _____

_____

9. After the lessons, Josh buys sodas for the children. _____

_____

10. In his free time, Josh writes special songs for his friends. _____

_____

At Christmas Practical Pete gives at least a small present to every one of his family members and acquaintances. Use the list of Pete's presents to answer the questions below. The first one has been done for you as an example.

MOM - DISH TOWELS
DAD - FLASHLIGHT
ANGELA + BOB - CAR WAX
BRAD - SOCKS
SECRETARY - DICTIONARY
CECELIA - Hairbrush
MAIL CARRIER - Dog Repellent
NEIGHBORS - Screwdriver Set

1. Who(m) does Pete give socks to?

   *Pete gives socks to Brad.*

2. What does Pete give the neighbors?

3. Who(m) does Pete give the hairbrush to?

4. What does Pete give the mail carrier?

5. What does Pete give his girlfriend?

6. Who(m) does Pete give the dictionary to?

7. What does Pete give to his dad?

8. Who(m) does Pete give the dish towels to?

9. Who(m) does Pete give the car wax to?

10. What does Pete give to his secretary?

11. Who(m) does Pete give the screwdriver set to?

## EXERCISE 7 (Focus 5)

Pete's gifts are always practical, but they aren't always the best gifts. What gifts do you think would be more appropriate? Write four sentences emphasizing what each person should receive and four sentences emphasizing who should receive each gift.

EXAMPLE: _Pete gives his mother some perfume._ (emphasis is on what)

**WHO**

1. _____

2. _____

3. _____

4. _____

**WHAT**

1. _____

2. _____

3. _____

4. _____

## EXERCISE 8 (Focus 6)

Change the sentences to pattern B (the indirect object goes before the direct object) if possible.

EXAMPLE: Josh says "thank you" to his friend. **no change**

Pete gives practical presents to his friends and family.

_Pete gives his friends and family practical presents._

1. I do the homework for my math teacher every day. _____

_____

2. I hand the homework to my teacher. _____

_____

3. The teacher explains the math problems for the students. _____

_____

4. He teaches algebra to the students. _____

_____

5. He introduces new mathematical concepts to the students. _____

_____

**6.** He shows the solution to the students. _____

_____

**7.** Angel offers help to Gretchen. _____

_____

**8.** He repeats the explanation for Gretchen. _____

_____

**9.** Angel solves the problem for Gretchen. _____

_____

**10.** Gretchen corrects her homework for the teacher. _____

_____

# UNIT 14

## Can, Know How To, Be Able To, And/But/So/Or

Mrs. and Mr. Sierra have just bought an apartment building. They want to rent it, but the building needs some repairs first. With the help of their daughter, Sisi, they plan to do many of the repairs. However, they must also hire a plumber, carpenter, and electrician to help them.

**Following is a list of the things they can do and the things they need help with. Write three sentences about each person—one sentence about what he or she *can't* do and two sentences about what he or she *can* do. The first one has been done for you.**

**MR. SIERRA**
scrape the old paint
repair the window screens

**MRS. SIERRA**
paint the walls
wallpaper the hallway

**PLUMBER**
fix the shower
install a hot-water heater

**CARPENTER**
build kitchen cabinets
repair the cracked plaster

**ELECTRICIAN**
install a ceiling fan
repair light switches

**SISI**
mow the grass
rake the leaves

**Mr. Sierra**

1. _____Mr. Sierra can't fix the shower._____
2. _____
3. _____

**Mrs. Sierra**

1. _____
2. _____
3. _____

**Carpenter**

1. _____
2. _____
3. _____

**Sisi**

1. _____
2. _____
3. _____

**Plumber**

1. _____
2. _____
3. _____

**Electrician**

1. _____
2. _____
3. _____

## EXERCISE 2 (Focus 2)

Look at the projects on the list in Exercise 1. With a partner, take turns asking who can do the things on the list. Be honest!

EXAMPLE: **A:** *Can you fix a shower?*

**B:** *No, I can't. (Yes, I can.)*

## EXERCISE 3 (Focus 2)

Take a survey: Ask three friends if they can do the activities listed below.

|  | NAME | NAME | NAME |
|---|---|---|---|
| 1. speak Cantonese | | | |
| 2. swim | | | |
| 3. drive a car | | | |
| 4. fix a flat tire | | | |
| 5. play a musical instrument | | | |
| 6. cook | | | |

## EXERCISE 4 (Focus 2)

Write questions for each of the answers given. Use the underlined words as cues.

EXAMPLE:  When can you visit me?

I can visit you <u>next week</u>.

1. _____

You can pick up the papers <u>after 6:00</u>.

2. _____

You can meet me <u>at the main entrance</u>.

3. _____

We can rent the TV camera <u>for five hours</u>.

4. _____

Your father can take the medicine <u>three times a day</u>.

5. _____

You can find the butter <u>next to the milk</u>.

**6.** _____

That's no problem, <u>my dad</u> can show you how to fix it.

**7.** _____

We can find the right size <u>at the new mall</u>.

**8.** _____

<u>I</u> can drive you to the store.

**9.** _____

<u>A good dictionary</u> can help you understand the words better.

**10.** _____

You can find the best fruit <u>in the summer</u>.

## EXERCISE 5  (Focus 3)

**With a partner, take turns asking if each of the following statements is correct in English. Correct any mistakes.**

EXAMPLE:　**A:** Can I say "My mother can cooks the best chicken and rice?"
　　　　　　**B:** No, You can't. The correct way to say that is "My mother can cook the best chicken and rice."

**1.** My mother can cooks the best chicken and rice.

**2.** I know how to breath.

**3.** You can speak English very well.

**4.** You can fishing from this bridge?

**5.** Do you know how to play a card game?

**6.** I can no finish in time.

## EXERCISE 6  (Focus 4)

**Read the following list. Make a check by each activity that is a learned ability.**

_____ laughing　　　　　　　　_____ reading

_____ speaking English　　　　 _____ seeing

_____ riding a bike　　　　　　 _____ crying

_____ hearing　　　　　　　　　_____ tasting

_____ flying an airplane　　　　_____ swimming

_____ smelling　　　　　　　　 _____ writing

**Answer the following questions.**

1. What is something you know how to do?_____

2. What is something you don't know how to do?_____

3. What is something you can do?_____

4. What is something you cannot do?_____

5. What is something you are able to do? _____

6. What is something you are not able to do? _____

Below is a list of things Ali can and can't do. Write sentences about Ali using *or, so,* *and,* or *but* as connectors. One has been done for you as an example.

| CAN | | CAN'T | |
|---|---|---|---|
| swim | ride a sled | dive | drive a snowmobile |
| float | drive a car | stay under water | repair the engine |
| paint | fix a flat tire | a long time | replace a broken |
| draw | wash clothes | make jewelry | headlight |
| ice skate | remove stains | make pottery | sew |
| | | ski | iron |

1. ___Ali can swim, but he can't stay under water a long time._____

2. _____

3. _____

4. _____

5. _____

6. _____

7. _____

8. _____

9. _____

10. _____

11. _____

12. _____

13. _____

14. _____

15. _____

# UNIT

# 15 Present Progressive Tense

---

**EXERCISE 1** *(Focus 1)*

Read the story and then complete the sentences that follow with the correct form of the present progressive tense. The first one has been done for you.

I am Jose Villanuevo. This is my family. I have three sisters. Jennifer is my older sister. My two younger sisters, Carmen and Margarita, are twins. I also have a younger brother, Tito, and a baby brother, Ricky. We are on vacation. Right now we are having fun at the Wild Water amusement park.

1. Jennifer __is looking_____ (look) at the lifeguard.

2. Tito _____ (eat) a hot dog.

3. The lifeguard _____ (watch) the swimmers and blowing his whistle.

4. Carmen and Margarita _____ (sit) in the sand.

5. The man _____ (jump) in the water.

6. Mom _____ (buy) the hot dogs and hamburgers.

7. Dad _____ (sleep) on the sand.

8. Ricky _____ (wade).

9. I _____ (slide) down the water slide.

10. The hot dogs _____ (burn).

11. The drinks _____ (spill).

## EXERCISE 2 (Focus 1)

Rewrite the sentences in Exercise 1 with a time expression at the beginning or end of each sentence. The first one has been done for you as an example.

1. _____Right now, Jennifer is looking at the lifeguard._____

or

_____Jennifer is looking at the lifeguard at the moment._____

2. _____

3. _____

4. _____

5. _____

6. _____

7. _____

8. _____

9. _____

10. _____

11. _____

## EXERCISE 3 (Focus 1)

Work with a partner. Take turns pointing to an activity in the picture in Exercise 1 and telling each other what's happening using a contraction.

## EXERCISE 4 (Focus 2)

Look at each of the pictures. Write a sentence describing each activity using the words in parentheses as cues. Be sure to spell each verb correctly and use the correct form. The first one has been done for you.

1. _____

(Ricky/wade)

2. _____

(Dad/get/sunburn)

3. _____

(Carmen/dig)

4. _____

(swimmers/splash)

5. _____

(the girls/bury/dad)

6. _____

(hot dogs/burn)

**7.** _____

_____

_____

(I/slide)

**8.** _____

_____

_____

(lifeguard/blow/whistle)

**9.** _____

_____

_____

(Dad/lie in sand)

**10.** _____

_____

_____

(Mom/buy/food)

**11.** _____

_____

_____

(Jennifer/flirt)

**12.** _____

_____

_____

(Tito/eat)

Now we're on our way home from the water park. Everyone is hot and tired, and we aren't having fun.

**Using the negative form, complete the sentences describing the picture. The first one has been done for you.**

1. Tito/feel well _Tito is not feeling well._ _____

   _____

2. The family/have fun _____

   _____

3. Dad/drive carefully_____

   _____

4. Carmen and Margarita/sit still _____

   _____

5. Mom/agree with Dad_____

   _____

6. The air conditioning/work_____

   _____

7. I/talk to my family _____

   _____

8. Traffic/move _____

   _____

9. Jennifer/smile _____

   _____

**10.** Ricky/sleep _____

_____

**11.** Dad/watch the road _____

_____

## EXERCISE 6 (Focus 3)

**Rewrite the sentences you wrote in Exercise 5 using negative contractions.**

EXAMPLE: *Tito isn't feeling well.* _____

1. _____
2. _____
3. _____
4. _____
5. _____
6. _____
7. _____
8. _____
9. _____
10. _____
11. _____

## EXERCISE 7 (Focus 3)

**Go to a busy place such as a mall or a supermarket and write ten affirmative or negative sentences about things you see people doing.**

EXAMPLE: *People are carrying shopping bags.* _____

1. _____
2. _____
3. _____
4. _____
5. _____
6. _____
7. _____
8. _____

**9.** _____

**10.** _____

## EXERCISE 8  (Focus 4)

**Complete each complex sentence below by adding a phrase in the simple present or the present progressive. Use _but_ to connect the two phrases. Be sure to use the correct time expression in your answer. The first one has been done for you as an example.**

At Christmas things are different around my house—we don't do the things that we usually do.

**1.** I usually go to school, _but today I'm shoveling snow._____

**2.** I'm usually in math class right now, _____

_____

**3.** _____ today he's putting up the Christmas lights.

**4.** Mom rarely makes cookies, _____

_____

**5.** _____ now she isn't at her boyfriend's house she's talking to him on the phone.

**6.** Ricky usually takes a nap,_____

_____ .

**7.** _____ at the moment he's eating cookies.

**8.** _____, at present they are arguing over a decoration.

**9.** Mom usually takes care of Ricky during the day, _____

_____

**10.** Dad usually helps me shovel the snow, _____

_____

**11.** Tito usually eats healthy food, _____

_____ .

## EXERCISE 9 (Focus 4)

Complete each of the following sentences by telling about an action that is temporary or a situation that is changing in your life. Then share some of the sentences you wrote with your classmates.

1. This week _____

_____

2. Today_____

_____

3. These days _____

_____

4. This month_____

_____

5. Nowadays_____

_____

6. This year_____

_____

## EXERCISE 10 (Focus 5)

Read the following sentences. Put both verbs at the end of the sentence in their correct places in the sentence. Be sure to use the correct form of each verb. The first one has been done for you.

1. Dad ____*seems*____ impatient; he ____*is honking*____ the horn. (honk, seem)

2. He _____ the bun, so he _____ the meat. (not eat, prefer)

3. That radio _____ wet; it _____ to me. (get, belong)

4. Mom    always    _____    where    she    put    her    keys;    then    she
_____ for them. (look, forget)

5. I _____ something funny; the hot dogs _____. (burn, smell)

6. I _____ a good job, but I _____ problems with my
boss. (have, have)

7. Tito _____ again; that boy _____ food. (love, eat)

8. The water park _____ nice; the kids _____ fun. (seem,
have)

9. The car _____ to dad, but he _____ trouble with the
air conditioning. (have, belong)

10. They _____ in God; that's why they _____ to church.
(go, believe)


## EXERCISE 11 (Focus 6)

Choose an appropriate verb and write a question for each set of words. Ask your
partner the questions and record his or her short answers.

EXAMPLE:    You/ other classes

A: _Are you taking other classes?_

B: _Yes, I am._

1. You / this class _____

_____

2. Your English / better _____

_____

3. You / your classmates _____

_____

4. You / English at home _____

_____

5. You / English grammar _____

_____

6. English grammar / easier _____

_____

7. You / good day _____

_____

8. I / questions correctly _____

_____

**9.** Your mother / in the United States _____

_____

**10.** I / clearly _____

_____

Now, we are getting ready for a big family reunion. There are so many people that Mom made a list of who is coming, what food they are bringing, when they are coming, how they are coming, and where they are sleeping. I hope they bring enough food for Tito!

**Look at the lists and write 15 questions about the people coming to the family reunion, using as many different question words as possible. Then answer the questions you write. There are many correct answers to this exercise. Compare your answers to those of your classmates.**

EXAMPLE:    *When are Grandma and Grandpa arriving?*

*They are arriving Friday morning.*


| WHO | WHAT | WHEN | HOW | WHERE |
|---|---|---|---|---|
| Grandma and Grandpa | potato salad | Friday morning | car | twins' room |
| Uncle Manuel | drinks | Friday 7:00 A.M. | train | living room |
| cousin Carla and her husband | fresh fruit | Friday noon | plane | Jose's room |
| Aunt Luz | cake | Friday evening | car | guest room |
| Uncle Raul | chips | Friday morning | bus | garage |

1. _____

_____

2. _____

_____

3. _____

_____

4. _____

_____

5. _____

_____

6. _____

_____

7. _____

_____

8. _____

_____

9. _____

_____

10. _____

_____

11. _____

_____

12. _____

_____

13. _____

_____

14. _____

_____

15. _____

_____

# Test Preparation Exercises
## Units 13–15

**Choose the *one* underlined word or phrase that best completes each sentence.**

1. _____ a musical instrument?
   - (A) Can you playing
   - (B) Can you play
   - (C) You can to play
   - (D) You play

2. I can sing, but I _____ play a musical instrument.
   - (A) canot
   - (B) can't
   - (C) no can
   - (D) can

3. Many of my friends play _____. I like to hear _____ sing.
   - (A) guitar...them
   - (B) guitars...they
   - (C) guitar...they
   - (D) guitars...them

4. Do they _____ play other instruments?
   - (A) can
   - (B) cannot
   - (C) know how to
   - (D) can't

5. My friend Simon also _____ the piano.
   - (A) is playing
   - (B) playing
   - (C) plays
   - (D) play

6. He _____ every day. In fact, he _____ right now.
   - (A) is practicing...practices
   - (B) practices...is practicing
   - (C) practice...is practicing
   - (D) practices...practicing

7. Where _____ every day?
   - (A) does he practicing
   - (B) he practices
   - (C) does he practice
   - (D) is he practicing

8. He _____ practices at his mother's house.
   - (A) right now
   - (B) at this moment
   - (C) nowadays
   - (D) usually

9. _____ he plays in an elegant bar.
   - (A) Now
   - (B) Tonight
   - (C) At this moment
   - (D) Every weekend

**10.** Simon _____ to play Spanish guitar music.
        (A) is preferring         (C) prefers
        (B) prefer         (D) is prefers

**11.** He _____ on some new songs now.
        (A) is working         (C) works
        (B) will work         (D) working

**12.** Right now he is playing guitar at the bar on the weekends, but he _____ guitar at the bar during the week.
        (A) 's not playing         (C) are not playing
        (B) is playing         (D) plays

**13.** _____ his job? Yes he _____.
        (A) Does he enjoy…is         (C) Are we enjoying…are
        (B) Is he enjoying…is         (D) Is he enjoy…is

**14.** His boss pays _____ pretty well.
        (A) he         (C) him
        (B) to him         (D) her

**15.** That's great—he can enjoy his work _____ a lot of money.
        (A) and make         (C) but can't make
        (B) but can make         (D) and cannot make

**Identify the *one* underlined word or phrase that must be changed for the sentence to be grammatically correct.**

**16.** We're going to the beach. Can Ellen come? Does she can swim?
     **A**    **B**             **C**       **D**

**17.** Ellen is afraid of water, but this week we are helping she to swim.
        **A**             **B**    **C**   **D**

**18.** Where is she taking lessons? At the pool; she is going there every day.
    **A**       **B**                **C**      **D**

**19.** Every morning she walks to the pool. She gives to me her towel. Then she puts her toe
     **A**           **B**            **C**            **D**
in the water.

**20.** At first she is hating the water, but once she jumps in she splashes happily.
            **A**        **B**        **C**          **D**

**21.** She can no swim perfectly, but she is learning. Now she can swim to her mother.
      **A**               **B**        **C**   **D**

**22.** She knows how to breathe. Now she is learning how to breathe when she is swimming.
        **A**        **B**    **C**                  **D**

**23.** She <u>can go</u> <u>to the beach</u>, but I always watch <u>she</u> carefully.
          A  B      C                         D

**24.** She <u>cannot</u> swim well. She <u>needs me</u> near <u>to her</u> when she <u>is swimming</u>.
             A                   B     C           D

**25.** We always <u>stay</u> in shallow water <u>and</u> we always <u>are watching</u> <u>her</u> and the other little
                  A               B          C   D

children.

**26.** <u>Can</u> your brother <u>makes</u> model airplanes? Yes, <u>this week</u> he <u>is building</u> a new model.
     A              B                      C      D

**27.** He <u>can put</u> the pieces together, <u>and</u> he <u>can't paint</u> the model by himself. He needs <u>me to</u>
       A                       B       C                                           

<u>help him</u>.
   D

**28.** <u>Who helping</u> <u>him</u> with this model? I <u>am helping</u> <u>him</u>.
     A        B                         C    D

**29.** First, before <u>he builds</u> a model, he <u>reads</u> all the directions. <u>He reads</u> <u>they</u> quickly.
                A               B                     C   D

**30.** Right now <u>I am helping</u> <u>her</u> do the difficult parts. <u>My brother and I</u> like to build <u>them</u>
               A       B                        C                     D

together.

# UNIT 16

# Adjective Phrases
## Another, The Other, Other(s),
## The Other(s) Intensifiers

Match the following sentences with the pictures they describe. The first one has been done for you.

a

d

e

b

c

1. The men in the ambulance are paramedics. __d__

2. The boy on the skateboard is going to crash. _____

3. The man at the stoplight is in a hurry. _____

4. The minivan on the highway is full of children. _____

5. The car with the red light on top is a police car. _____

6. The tricycle with the squeaky wheel belongs to the little girl. _____

7. The van parked at the grocery store is full of bread. _____

8. The fire engine with the ladder is blocking the intersection. _____

9. The bulldozer with the woman driver is new. _____

10. The car with a dent is a sports car. _____

11. The elegant lady with the chauffeur owns a limousine. _____

f          g          h

i          j          k

## EXERCISE 2    (Focus 1)

Circle the adjective phrases in each of the sentences in Exercise 1.

## EXERCISE 3    (Focus 1)

Each vehicle on page 124 belongs to one of the people shown on the page. Match each person to the appropriate vehicle. Then write sentences using adjective phrases. The first one has been done for you.

*The woman with all the children drives the van.*

1. _____

2. _____

3. _____

4. _____

5. _____

6. _____

7. _____

8. _____

9. _____

10. _____

11. _____

A

B

C

D

E

F

G

H

I

J

K

**Cheryl and her daughter Rachel are shopping for school clothes. They each have different ideas about what kind of clothes Rachel should wear. Complete the following by writing *which* questions for each answer.**

1. _____

Cheryl wants to get the long skirt.

2. _____

Rachel likes the high-heeled shoes.

3. _____

Rachel prefers long, dangling earrings.

4. _____

Cheryl wants to buy the pullover sweater.

5. _____

Rachel likes the skirt with holes.

6. _____

Cheryl prefers the small earrings.

7. _____

Rachel likes the tight blouse.

8. _____

Rachel wants to buy the hooded sweater.

9. _____

Cheryl wants to buy the flat shoes.

These are the new school clothes Cheryl bought for Rachel. Take turns with a partner, asking which clothes they bought.

EXAMPLE:    **A:** *Which earrings did they buy?*

**B:** *They bought the small ones.*

Complete the following story with *another, the other(s),* or *other(s).* The first one has been done for you as an example.

How do astronauts live in space? One problem of living in space is how to keep the astronauts warm. _____*Other*_____ problems are eating, sleeping, and exercising with no gravity. The outside of the space shuttle is covered with small tiles. Under the tiles there are _____ layers of metal to protect the astronauts from the cold of space.

How do they eat? Some of the food on the space shuttle is in small pieces. The astronauts eat that food through a straw. But they eat _____ foods, such as meat, whole. _____ kind of food they eat whole is fruit. _____ foods that astronauts eat include shrimp, steak, and broccoli. Besides candy, _____ dessert is ice cream.

_____ problem for astronauts is sleeping. Some astronauts sleep standing up, while _____ sleep lying down. Astronauts sleep tied to their beds so they don't float around. While one astronaut sleeps, _____ work or exercise. There are two reasons why the astronauts exercise. One reason is to stay in shape; _____ reason is because their muscles get weak in space.

**Think about the following subjects and rate them on the continuum using the adjectives provided. Then write two sentences, one positive and one negative. Use an intensifier in each sentence.**

EXAMPLE:   The English language

difficult ................................................................ **X** ............... easy

*The English language is fairly easy.*

*The English language isn't very difficult.*

1. algebra

difficult .................................................................................................... easy

_____

_____

2. a Rolls Royce

elegant .................................................................................................... plain

_____

_____

3. horror films

frightening ............................................................................................... funny

_____

_____

4. Antarctica

warm ....................................................................................................... cold

_____

_____

5. The Mediterranean

clean .................................................................................................. polluted

_____

_____

6. Moscow

large ...................................................................................................... small

_____

_____

7. airplanes

loud ....................................................................................................... quiet

_____

_____

# UNIT 17

# Past Tense of Be

Match the people and places in the first column with the descriptions in the second column. Then, using that information, write sentences. The first one has been done for you as an example.

| | | |
|---|---|---|
| **1.** the Marx Brothers | _____ | a French general |
| **2.** Ernest Hemingway and Mark Twain | _____ | an Olympic boxer |
| **3.** Napoleon Bonaparte | _____ | African Nations |
| **4.** Winston Churchill | _____ | eastern European nations |
| **5.** the Soviet Union and East Germany | _1_ | a comedy team |
| **6.** Eva Peron | _____ | American rock singers |
| **7.** Muhammad Ali | _____ | a British prime minister |
| **8.** Rhodesia and Upper Volta | _____ | a professional tennis player |
| **9.** Arthur Ashe | _____ | American writers |
| **10.** Elvis Presley, Jimi Hendrix, and Jim Morrison | _____ | the wife of the president of Argentina |

1.  The Marx Brothers were a comedy team. _____

2.  _____
    _____

3.  _____
    _____

4.  _____
    _____

5.  _____
    _____

6.  _____
    _____

7. _____

_____

8. _____

_____

9. _____

_____

10. _____

_____

**EXERCISE 2**  (*Focus 1*)

Tell a partner three things you felt when you first arrived in the United States or Canada. Then tell the rest of your classmates how your partner felt. Use the word list to help you.

EXAMPLE:    You tell your partner:

*I was afraid when I first arrived in Canada.*

Your partner tells the class:

*She was afraid.*

**WORD LIST**

| | | | | |
|---|---|---|---|---|
| upset | excited | tired | interested | mad |
| happy | angry | frightened | nervous | shy |
| afraid | sad | | | |

**EXERCISE 3**  (*Focuses 1 and 2*)

Using the cues, write true statements about life 100 years ago.

EXAMPLE:    expressways: ___There weren't any expressways 100 years ago.___

1. trains _____

_____

2. horses _____

_____

3. jet airplanes _____

_____

4. skate boards _____

_____

5. United Nations _____

_____

**6.** a country called China _____

_____

**7.** two countries on the Korean peninsula _____

_____

**8.** Olympic Games _____

_____

**9.** computers _____

_____

**10.** a prime minister of Canada _____

_____

**11.** a king or queen of Great Britain _____

_____

**12.** a president of the United States _____

_____


**EXERCISE 4** (*Focus 3*)

**Find out about your partner. Write sentences to ask what she or he was like as child. Check "yes" or "no" depending on his or her answer to each question.**

EXAMPLE:   <u>Were you neat when you were a child?</u> _____

Partner's name _____

|  | YES | NO |
|---|---|---|
| **1.** neat | _____ | _____ |
| **2.** helpful | _____ | _____ |
| **3.** happy | _____ | _____ |
| **4.** sad | _____ | _____ |
| **5.** good in school | _____ | _____ |
| **6.** funny | _____ | _____ |
| **7.** messy | _____ | _____ |

**1.** _____

**2.** _____

**3.** _____

**4.** _____

**5.** _____

**6.** _____

**7.** _____

**Write the question for each answer using the underlined words as cues.**

EXAMPLE:   *What was the name of Zimbabwe?*
_____

The name of Zimbabwe was <u>Rhodesia</u>.

**1.** _____

Eva Peron was from <u>Argentina</u>.

**2.** _____

<u>Mark Twain</u> was the author of *Tom Sawyer*.

**3.** _____

Muhammad Ali was in the Olympics <u>in 1960</u>.

**4.** _____

Rhodesia and Upper Volta were <u>African nations</u>.

**5.** _____

<u>Elvis Presley's</u> house was in Tennessee.

**6.** _____

Ernest Hemingway was born <u>in 1899.</u>

**7.** _____

The Soviet Union and East Germany were in <u>eastern Europe</u>

**8.** _____

Napoleon was arrested <u>because he supported the French Revolution</u>.

**9.** _____

<u>*Animal Crackers*</u> was one of the Marx Brothers' movies.

**10.** _____

Winston Churchill was prime minister of Great Britain <u>during World War II.</u>

# UNIT

# 18 Past Tense

Complete the story with the past-tense form of each verb in parentheses. Check your spelling. The first one has been done for you.

Bernie Bungle _____tried_____ (try) to rob the Midnight Market, but Bernie was not a very good robber. This is what happened to him.

Bernie _____ (plan) to rob the store early in the morning, but he overslept so he _____ (arrive) late.

When he got to the store he _____ (study) the cashier and customers carefully to make sure there were no police. Then he _____ (cover) his face with a nylon stocking, but the stocking was too thick so he couldn't see very well. That is why he _____ (trip) when he _____ (enter) the store. All the customers _____ (turn) and _____ (look) at him.

Bernie _____ (point) his gun at the cashier and _____ (demand) all the money. The cashier _____ (fill) up a bag with money and _____ (hand) it to Bernie.

After he _____ (rob) the store, Bernie _____ (try) to escape, but the money bag _____ (rip) and some of the money _____ (drop) out of the bag. When Bernie _____ (hop) into his car, he _____ (remember) why he _____ (want) to rob the store early in the morning. There was a traffic jam and he couldn't go anywhere.

The police _____ (worry) that the robber would get away. But when they _____ (arrive) there was Bernie, only one block away.

**(Focus 2)**

Your teacher will read the following words to you. Listen to the end sound. Put each word in the correct column depending on its end sound.

| AT SCHOOL | AT WORK | AT HOME | AT THE PLAYGROUND |
|---|---|---|---|
| learned | walked | vacuumed | played |
| discussed | delivered | polished | bounced |
| studied | fixed | ironed | jumped |
| answered | locked | changed | tripped |
| listened | worked | cleaned | enjoyed |
| named | started | baked | climbed |
| remembered | filed | washed | skated |
| corrected | pointed | dusted | skipped |
| printed | typed | brushed | hopped |
| asked | talked | scrubbed | kissed |

| GROUP 1 /T/ | GROUP 2 /D/ | GROUP 3 /ID/ |
|---|---|---|
| _____ | _____ | _____ |
| _____ | _____ | _____ |
| _____ | _____ | _____ |
| _____ | _____ | _____ |
| _____ | _____ | _____ |
| _____ | _____ | _____ |
| _____ | _____ | _____ |
| _____ | _____ | _____ |
| _____ | _____ | _____ |
| _____ | _____ | _____ |
| _____ | _____ | _____ |
| _____ | _____ | _____ |
| _____ | _____ | _____ |
| _____ | _____ | _____ |
| _____ | _____ | _____ |
| _____ | _____ | _____ |
| _____ | _____ | _____ |
| _____ | _____ | _____ |

## EXERCISE 3 (Focus 2)

With the other members of your group, make a past-tense chain story using one of the groups of verbs on page 132. To make a chain story, one member of the group starts the story. After he or she says one of the words from the list, the next person in the group continues the story. Each person in the group adds to the story. Make sure that each member of the group pronounces the past tense verb correctly.

EXAMPLE: **First student:** *When I was in elementary school, I **studied** math.*

**Second student:** *I liked math. I **answered** all the questions…*

**Third student:** *and I always **listened** to the teacher. (etc.)*

## EXERCISE 4 (Focus 3)

Complete the story with the past-tense form of each verb in parentheses. The first one has been done for you.

As soon as Bernie Bungle ____got____ (get) out of jail for robbing the Midnight Market, he _____ (get) in trouble again. Bernie _____ (see) a house. It _____ (look) like no one was home. Bernie _____ (break) the window and _____ (go) in. He _____ (look) for something to steal. Bernie _____ (find) some jewelry and he _____ (put) it into a pillow case. As he _____ (look) around for something else to steal, he _____ (begin) to feel hungry. So he _____ (take) a look in the kitchen. He _____ (find) a frozen pizza and some beer. Bernie _____ (heat) the pizza and _____ (make) himself some lunch. He _____ (eat) the pizza and _____ (drink) all the beer. Then Bernie _____ (feel) a little tired, so he _____ (sit) down and _____ (fall) asleep. As he _____ (sleep), Mr. Chan _____ (come) home. When he _____ (see) Bernie sleeping in the chair, Mr. Chan _____ (call) the police. Bernie _____ (hear) him and _____ (wake) up. He _____ (stand) up and _____ (run) out of the house. However, the police _____ (catch) Bernie on his way out. He _____ (go) to jail again.

Today is October 31. David Johnson is the gardener at Pine Cone College. He has a busy schedule. The calendar shows what he did in the last month. Write a sentence about the calendar for each of the cues below. The first one has been done for you.

| Sunday | Monday | Tuesday | Wednesday | Thursday | Friday | Saturday |
|---|---|---|---|---|---|---|
| 29 | 30 | 1 *rake leaves* | 2 *mow grass* | 3 *trim hedges* | 4 *fertilize trees* | 5 |
| 6 | 7 *trim trees* | 8 *rake leaves* | 9 *mow grass* | 10 *repair sprinklers* | 11 *spray for insects* | 12 |
| 13 | 14 *repair equipment* | 15 *rake leaves* | 16 *mow grass* | 17 *trim hedges* | 18 | 19 |
| 20 | 21 | 22 *rake leaves* | 23 *mow grass* | 24 *plant flowers* | 25 *repair sprinklers* | 26 |
| 27 | 28 *check tools* | 29 *rake leaves* | 30 *morning trim hedges* / *afternoon mow grass* / *night set up president's party* | 31 | 1 | 2 |

1. (yesterday)

   David trimmed the hedges, mowed the grass, and set up for the party yesterday.

   or

   Yesterday, David trimmed the hedges, mowed the grass, and set up for the party.

2. (last week)

   _____

   _____

3. (two days ago)

   _____

   _____

4. (on Monday)

   _____

   _____

5. (yesterday morning)

   _____

   _____

**6.** (last night)

_____

_____

**7.** (the day before yesterday)

_____

_____

**8.** (two weeks ago)

_____

_____

**9.** (last Friday)

_____

_____

**10.** (yesterday afternoon)

_____

_____


## EXERCISE 6    (Focus 4)

**Write a sentence telling what you did at the times or dates given.**

EXAMPLE:    yesterday afternoon

_Yesterday afternoon I went out for lunch._

OR

_I went out for lunch yesterday afternoon._

**1.** yesterday afternoon

_____

_____

**2.** last night

_____

_____

**3.** last weekend

_____

_____

**4.** six months ago

_____

_____

**5.** last year

_____

_____

**6.** the day before yesterday

_____

_____

**7.** an hour ago

_____

_____

**8.** last month

_____

_____

## EXERCISE 7    (*Focus 5*)

**Make each of the following statements true by using the negative form in the past tense. The first one has been done for you.**

1. Bernie woke up on time on the day he robbed the Midnight Market.

   _Bernie didn't wake up on time the day he robbed the Midnight Market._

   _____

2. Bernie wore a ski mask on his head.

   _____

   _____

3. Bernie got away after he robbed the Midnight Market.

   _____

   _____

4. Bernie learned his lesson after robbing the Midnight Market.

   _____

   _____

5. Bernie opened the window when he robbed Mr. Chan's house.

   _____

   _____

**6.** Bernie bought some jewelry at the store.

_____

_____

**7.** Bernie stole Mr. Chan's TV.

_____

_____

**8.** Bernie ate a sandwich.

_____

_____

**9.** Bernie drank some coffee.

_____

_____

**10.** Bernie slept in a bed.

_____

_____

**11.** Mr. Chan called the fire department.

_____

_____

**12.** Bernie drove away in his car from Mr. Chan's house.

_____

_____

**13.** Bernie escaped from the police two times.

_____

_____

**(Focus 6)**

**Can you remember what you did when you were in elementary school? Using the cues, take turns with your partner asking about each other's early school experience. Write down your partner's short answers.**

EXAMPLE:   **A:** *Did you wear a uniform to school?*

**B:** *Yes, I did. (No, I didn't.)*

**Ask your partner if he or she:**

1. wore a uniform to school _____

2. helped the teacher _____

3. studied hard _____

4. rode a bus to school _____

5. got good grades _____

6. sang songs in school _____

7. liked his or her teachers _____

8. played sports _____

9. his or her parents bought his or her books _____

10. said "good morning" to the teacher _____

**EXERCISE 9**   **(Focus 7)**

**Imagine you are a newspaper reporter. You heard the story about Bernie Bungle, the burglar. You want to ask the victims questions about Bernie's two crimes. Use the question words and cues to write the questions you want to ask. The first one has been done for you.**

## THE CASHIER AT THE MIDNIGHT MARKET

1. Why / Bernie / trip

   *Why did Bernie trip when he entered the store?* _____

2. Where/you/put money

   _____

3. What / happen / to the money

   _____

4. What / police / do

   _____

5. Where / police / catch

   _____

**MR. CHAN**

**6.** What / happen

_____

**7.** How / he / get in

_____

**8.** Who / find him

_____

**9.** Where / you / find him

_____

**10.** What / you / do

_____

**11.** How long / he / sleep

_____

# TOEFL®

## Test Preparation Exercises
### Units 16–18

**Choose the *one* word or phrase that best completes each sentence.**

1. _____ do last night?
   - (A) What you did
   - (B) Did you
   - (C) What did you
   - (D) You did

2. Last night I _____ my mother.
   - (A) visited
   - (B) visit
   - (C) am visiting
   - (D) visits

3. _____ dinner at her house? Yes I did.
   - (A) What did you eat
   - (B) What were you
   - (C) Did you ate
   - (D) Did you eat

4. Yesterday my mother _____ spaghetti for dinner. It _____ delicious.
   - (A) maked…were
   - (B) made…were
   - (C) makes…is
   - (D) made…was

5. _____ your mother?
   - (A) Which
   - (B) Which one is
   - (C) Which are
   - (D) Which was

6. The woman _____ my mother.
   - (A) in the polka dot dress is
   - (B) in polka dot dress is
   - (C) with the frying pan works
   - (D) with frying pan is being

7. She's great. Last night she also _____ my clothes, but she _____ them for me.
   - (A) washed . . . ironed
   - (B) washed…didn't iron
   - (C) didn't wash…didn't iron
   - (D) washed…didn't ironed

8. _____ I wasn't living in North America.
   - (A) Three months ago
   - (B) Three last months
   - (C) At three months ago
   - (D) In three months ago

9. Last year I _____ Russia.
   - (A) leave
   - (B) am leaving
   - (C) leaved
   - (D) left

10. The U.S. government _____ me to this country when an American family _____ to sponsor me last winter.
    (A) admited…agreeed     (C) admit…agree
    (B) admits…agrees     (D) admitted…agreed

11. The Rosenburg family _____ me money last year.
    (A) sends     (C) sent
    (B) is sending     (D) was

12. When I first _____ to the United States I _____ happy.
    (A) came…wasn't     (C) did come…were not
    (B) came…didn't be     (D) come…weren't

13. Mr. Rosenburg, _____, was very kind to me.
    (A) that man with mustache     (C) that mustache man
    (B) that man with the mustache     (D) that man in the mustache

14. In the beginning, I _____ letters to my family every day.
    (A) write     (C) writed
    (B) wrote     (D) was write

15. _____ problem I had was with the food.
    (A) Other     (C) Others
    (B) Another     (D) Anothers

**Identify the *one* underlined word or phrase that must be changed for the sentence to be grammatically correct.**

16. What did she taught in grammar class yesterday?
    A    B    C        D

17. What grammar class are you talking about, the morning or the afternoon class? The
    A                B    C
one in the morning.
    D

18. Yesterday morning the lesson is easy. We reviewed past-tense verbs and practiced using
    A                B           C                   D
the verbs in sentences.

19. Other grammar class was more difficult. I didn't understand everything.
    A                B           C    D

20. Where were you yesterday? I no see you at school.
    A    B    C      D

21. I was absent because I was very sick. I haved a stomachache.
    A                B    C    D

**22.** <u>What did make</u> <u>you sick</u>? The <u>night before last</u> I <u>ate</u> something bad and I got food
      A            B                    C        D
poisoning.

**23.** I <u>was</u> so sick, it <u>was</u> terrible. Finally, I <u>told</u> my dad that I <u>wasn't</u> feel well.
       A             B               C           D

**24.** My doctor <u>wasn't</u> in so I <u>had</u> to see <u>another</u> doctor. The new doctor <u>in clinic</u> helped me a
             A         B        C                 D
lot.

**25.** I <u>described</u> the problem and he <u>gave</u> me some medicine. <u>Did the medicine help</u>?
      A                      B                    C
<u>Yes, it didn't.</u>
     D

**26.** He <u>prescribed</u> two kinds of medicine. <u>One</u> <u>was</u> a pink liquid and <u>the others</u> was a pill.
        A                         B  C             D

**27.** <u>The same thing</u> <u>happened</u> to me <u>last year ago</u>, but I <u>had</u> to go to the hospital.
        A        B           C        D

**28.** <u>That's</u> terrible! You <u>were</u> really sick. <u>How long you stayed</u> in the hospital? I <u>was</u> there only
      A         B                C              D
one day.

**29.** <u>The another</u> problem <u>was</u> I <u>didn't know</u> how I was going <u>to pay</u> the hospital bill.
      A            B    C              D

**30.** My uncle <u>offered</u> to help me. <u>Which uncle is that</u>? My uncle <u>with the big house</u> <u>help</u> me
           A                     B                C     D
pay some of the bills.

# UNIT 19

# Reflexive Pronouns, Reciprocal Pronoun: *Each Other*

## EXERCISE 1    (*Focus 1*)

Write the correct reflexive pronoun in each of the spaces provided in the dialogue. The first one has been done for you.

Paul and Charlotte are having a Halloween party. For the first time, they are putting on a party all by ___ themselves ___. They are a little nervous.

**Charlotte:** Are you okay? What happened?

**Paul:** I'm fine. I just cut _____ a little when I was carving the jack-o'-lantern.

**Charlotte:** You should wash that cut and get _____ a bandage.

**Paul:** Okay. Should I put the jack-o'-lantern by the ghost decoration?

**Charlotte:** No, put it over there alone, by _____. It will look more scary. How do you like my spider web decorations? I made them all by

_____.

**Paul:** Great! They look frightening. This is going to be a fun party. I hope the guests enjoy

_____.

**144**    Unit 19

**Charlotte:** I'm sure everyone will have fun. By the way, who's Brad bringing?

**Paul:** He couldn't find a date. I guess he's coming by _____.

**Charlotte:** Well, make sure you pay attention to the other guests too. Sometimes you and Brad go off by _____.

**Paul:** Don't worry. I'll spend time with the guests.

**Charlotte:** Do you think I should pour the drinks now or let the guests help _____?

**Paul:** Just let them help _____. I hope the guests arrive soon. I don't want us to have to eat all this food by _____.

**Charlotte:** They'll be here soon. Oh, we aren't in our costumes yet. We have to get _____ ready. Will you help me with my costume? I can't zip it up by _____.

## EXERCISE 2    (Focus 2)

**Decide if each of the following blanks requires a reflexive pronoun. If it does, write the correct pronoun in the space. If it doesn't, put an X in the space.**

*The story continues:*

**Charlotte:** I'm all dirty from making those spider webs. First I think I'll shower _____ and after I dry _____ you can help me with the zipper.

**Paul:** Okay While you're doing that I'll shave _____ and then dress _____.

**Charlotte:** What if the guests arrive early?

**Paul:** We can't blame _____ if they arrive early. I'm sure they can introduce _____. It won't take us long to dress _____.

*Later...*

**Paul:** See, I told you the guests would enjoy _____. Everyone is dancing and laughing. It looks like Brad has even found _____ a date. I knew he wouldn't have to be all by _____.

**Charlotte:** You're right, they are all amusing _____. This is a great costume party. Look at Cindy's costume.

**Paul:** What is she? She looks like she killed _____.

**Charlotte:** She's the bride of Frankenstein.

## EXERCISE 3   (Focus 2)

**Discuss with your partner the following items, using reflexive pronouns.**

EXAMPLE:   a holiday your family celebrates without inviting others

*We celebrate Christmas by ourselves.*

1. a holiday your family celebrates without inviting others
2. something you want to do by yourself
3. something you can do by yourself
4. something you think a husband or wife can do without his or her partner
5. a place you do not want to visit alone

**Tell the group your partner's answers.**

EXAMPLE:   You say:  *I can fix my car by myself.*

Your partner says:  *She can fix her car by herself.*

**Match each picture with the sentence that describes it. The first one has been done for you.**

1. The children are spraying themselves with water.

2. The children are spraying each other with water.

3. They are spinning themselves around.

4. They are spinning each other around.

5. They're hot. They are fanning themselves.

6. They're hot. They are fanning each other.

7. They are putting makeup on themselves.

8. They are putting makeup on each other.

9. They are washing their faces.

10. They are washing each other.

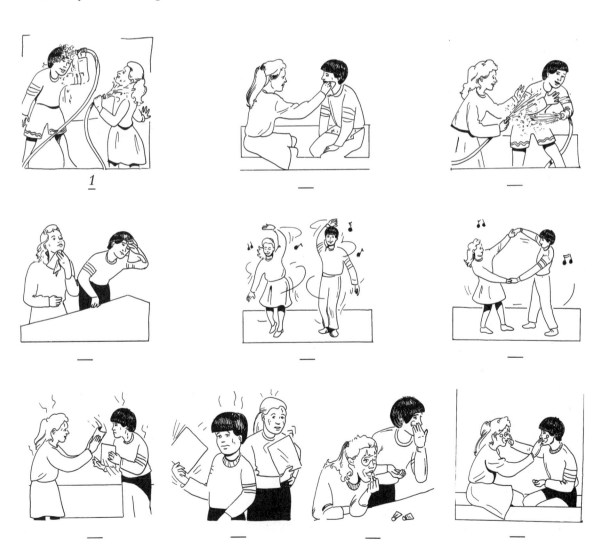

# UNIT

# 20 Future Time

## Will and Be Going To, May and Might

**EXERCISE 1** *(Focus 1)*

Clumsy Claire reads her horoscope every day. For the past week her horoscope has come true. Match the picture with the day the prediction appeared. Then match what Claire thought when her horoscope came true. Write it under the picture. The first one has been done for you.

**HOROSCOPES:**

Sunday: You'll get to see nature up close.

Monday: You will buy a new car.

Tuesday: Time will stand still for you.

Wednesday: This will be your lucky day!

Thursday: You will go on a trip.

Friday: A stranger will sweep you off your feet.

Saturday: You'll meet a new love interest.

**WHAT CLAIRE THOUGHT:**

My knee is going to hurt!

I'm going to need a new watch.

He's going to think I'm clumsy.

My car insurance is going to increase.

I'm going to call the exterminator.

I'm going to break my arm.

I'm going to put my lottery ticket in a safe place.

Tuesday: Time will stand still for you.
I'm going to need a new watch.

Read the horoscope section in a newspaper or magazine. Circle the words in the horoscopes that predict future events. Share the horoscopes with your classmates.

Here are some yearbook pictures of seniors at Hilly High School. Read the yearbook captions and then write two predictions of what each person will do in the future. The first one has been done for you as an example.

### ALICIA COOPER

**Dream:**
To sing in a rock band
**Favorite activity:**
playing my guitar

### ALBERTA EINSTEIN

**Dream:**
To win the Nobel prize
for science
**Favorite activity:**
physics experiments

### DANA MARINO

**Dream:**
To play football
in the NFL
**Favorite activity:**
sports

### GRACE GUNN

**Dream:**
To own a 1957 Chevy
**Favorite activity:**
repairing my car

### CLARA KLUTZ

**Dream:**
To dance in the New
York City Ballet
**Favorite activity:**
ballet dancing

### ROSS PARROT

**Dream:**
To make a million dollars
**Favorite activity:**
helping with my
dad's business

### CON STRUCTOR

**Dream:**
To build my own house
**Favorite activity:**
carpentry

### BRIAN TUMOR

**Dream:**
To find a cure for cancer
**Favorite activity:**
volunteering at the hospital

### CULL T. VATOR

**Dream:**
To own my own land
in the country
**Favorite activity:**
growing plants.

Alicia

1. <u>Alicia will meet some other musicians.</u>

2. _____

Alberta

3. _____

4. _____

Dana

5. _____

6. _____

Grace

7. _____

8. _____

Clara

9. _____

10. _____

Ross

11. _____

12. _____

Con

13. _____

14. _____

Brian

15. _____

16. _____

Cull

17. _____

18. _____


**EXERCISE 4**  (Focus 2)

Write the questions for each of the answers given using the underlined words as cues. The first one has been done for you.

1. <u>Will Ross own oil wells?</u>

<u>Yes</u>, Ross'll own oil wells.

**2.** _____

Alberta will win the Nobel Prize for science <u>in 2021</u>.

**3.** _____

Grace will open her garage <u>in town</u>.

**4.** _____

<u>No</u>, Clara will not become rich and famous.

**5.** _____

Cull will buy a tractor <u>because it will help him on the farm</u>.

**6.** _____

Brian will go to medical school <u>in Boston</u>.

**7.** _____

It'll take Con <u>one year</u> to build his new house.

**8.** _____

Dana will play football <u>in Miami</u>.

**9.** _____

<u>A famous agent</u> will discover Alicia.

## EXERCISE 5    (*Focus 3*)

**Complete the dialogue with the correct form of *be going to*. The first one has been done for you.**

**Helen:** <u>Are you going to</u> get ready for the party?

**Paul:** I don't want to. It _____ be fun at all. This _____ be a boring party.

**Helen:** It _____. It _____ be fun.

**Paul:** Your uncle _____ to want to show his vacation slides. The slides _____ put me asleep. Then we _____ listen to him talk about everything in detail. What _____ eat for dinner?

**Helen:** We _____ have roast beef.

**Paul:** It _____ be undercooked. I _____ to eat the meat if it is too rare. Your aunt _____ eat it then she _____ to feel well. I know she _____ get sick.

## EXERCISE 6 (Focus 3)

**Ask your partner to predict the following things. Be sure to use the correct form of** *going to* **in your questions and answers.**

EXAMPLE: Predict the weather tomorrow.

**A:** *What is the weather going to be like tomorrow?*

**B:** *It's going to rain.*

1. Predict what grade you are going to get in this class.
2. Predict when the sun is going to set tonight.
3. Predict who is going to be the next person to walk into your classroom.

## EXERCISE 7 (Focus 4)

**Look at Suzy's appointment calendar. Today is September first. Use the future time expression to tell when Suzy will do each of the following activities. The first one has been done for you.**

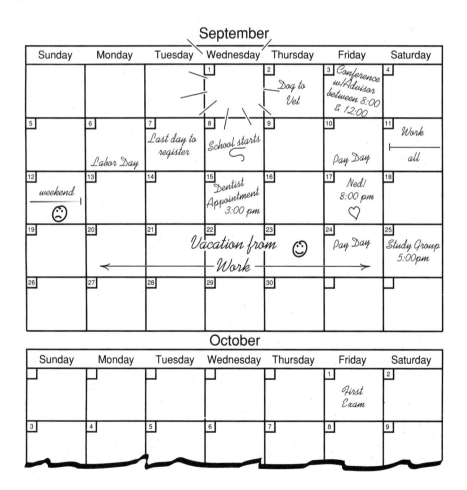

1. Start school  *Next week Suzy will start school.* _____

_____

2. Meet with her study group _____

_____

3. Have a dental appointment _____

_____

4. Get paid _____

_____

5. Have a vacation from work _____

_____

6. Have a conference with her advisor_____

_____

7. Have a date with Ned _____

_____

8. Take her first exam _____

_____

9. Have to take her dog to the vet _____

_____

10. Have to work all weekend_____

_____


## EXERCISE 8    (Focus 4)

**Look at Suzy's calendar again. Then answer the following questions.**

1. What time does the study group meet? _____

_____

2. How long is Suzy's vacation from work? _____

_____

3. What month will she start school? _____

_____

4. What night will she have a date with Ned? _____

_____

5. What time is her dental appointment?_____

_____

**6.** At what time should she see her advisor? _____

_____

**7.** How long is it until school begins?_____

_____

**8.** How long is it until she has to work all weekend?_____

_____

**9.** What day will she take her dog to the vet?_____

_____

**10.** Until what day can she register for classes?_____

_____

**EXERCISE 9** *(Focus 5)*

**Complete the dialogue with the correct form of *will* or *going to*. The first one has been done for you.**

**Aunt Polly:** Tom Sawyer, you ____*are going to*____ paint the

fence, that is already decided.

**Tom:** But Aunt Polly, I don't want to paint the fence.

**Aunt Polly:** I _____ stand for this Tom. You

_____ cause my death yet.

You _____ do some work.

**Tom:** But all the other boys _____ go swimming.

**Aunt Polly:** Well, you _____ do some painting.

**Ben:** Why are you carrying that bucket and brush, Tom? What _____ to do?

**Tom:** I _____ paint the fence.

**Ben:** Why _____ to do that? I _____ go swimming.

You _____ have any fun.

**Tom:** Because I like to. I _____ to have fun.

**Ben:** Hey, that looks like fun, let me try doing it.

**Tom:** No, Aunt Polly _____ like that.

Besides I'm having fun.

**Ben:** Please, Tom, let me do it?

**Tom:** Okay, but what _____ give me?

**Ben:** How about this apple?

**Tom:** Okay.

## EXERCISE 10 (Focus 5)

Read the dialogue again. Write P above the answers which predict future events and I above the answers which express intentions or prior plans.

## EXERCISE 11 (Focus 6)

What is possible for you in the next year? Write a sentence using affirmative or negative statements and *be going to, will, may* or *might* to describe your possible future actions.

EXAMPLE:  get a new pet ___I might get a new pet in the next year. (a possibility)___

___I'm not going to get a new pet in the next year.___

___(100% sure that it is not going to happen)___

1. get a new pet _____

_____

2. move to a new house or apartment_____

_____

3. finish taking English classes _____

_____

4. win the lottery_____

_____

5. get married_____

_____

6. take a vacation_____

_____

7. read a novel _____

_____

8. get a better job _____

_____

9. be in a car accident_____

_____

10. make a new friend _____

_____

## EXERCISE 12 (Focus 6)

Share your responses to Exercise 11 with a partner. Explain why you chose "possibility" for some and "certainty" for others.

# UNIT 21 Phrasal Verbs

---

**EXERCISE 1** (Focus 1)

**Read the following story. Circle the phrasal verbs. The first one has been done for you.**

My name is Jacques Desire. I am from Haiti. I want to be a journalist, but before I can study my major I have to improve my English.

Today I went to my first college class. I was a little nervous on my way to class. I drove a little too fast. I almost ran into another car. I told myself to calm down and slow down. Finally, I made it to class safely.

When I found the right classroom, I saw several students sitting in small groups. "Come in," said one Hispanic woman.

After I sat down the teacher came in. Immediately I stood up, but I couldn't figure it out. None of the other students stood up. In Haiti we always stand up when the teacher comes into the room. "Please sit down," said the teacher in a kind voice.

Then the teacher handed out some information cards. "Please fill out the card," she said, "and don't forget to write your phone number so I can call you up if I need to."

After we filled it out, the teacher handed out an information sheet about the course. She went over the requirements of the class and told us to put the information sheet away in a safe place.

---

**EXERCISE 2** (Focus 2)

**Write captions for the pictures about Jacques Desire's day. Use the following verbs to help you. The first one has been done for you.**

| hand out | come in | stand up | run into |
| fill out | go over | calm down | |

Jacques almost ran into another car.

_____

_____

_____

_____

_____

_____

_____

_____

_____

_____

_____

_____

_____

_____

_____

**Rewrite each of the following sentences two different ways, once with a noun and once with a pronoun. Follow the example.**

EXAMPLE:    The janitor cleans up the papers.

_He cleans the papers up._

_He cleans them up._

He takes out the trash.

1. _____

2. _____

He throws away the trash.

3. _____

4. _____

It is time to turn off the TV.

5. _____

6. _____

Please come in. Take off your coat.

7. _____

8. _____

I will hang up your coat.

9. _____

10. _____

Rewrite the two stories, replacing the underlined words with phrasal verbs. The first two sentences have been done for you as an example.

The house was a mess. Hazel dressed herself with her apron. First she collected all the trash and put it in the garbage. Then she collected all the dirty dishes. She cleaned the kitchen. Next she washed all the family's dirty clothes. She folded them and put the clothes in their usual place— she placed on a hanger all of the shirts, blouses, and dresses. Then she vacuumed the rugs. By the time she pulled the plug on the vacuum cleaner she was exhausted.

EXAMPLE:    The house was a mess. Hazel put on her apron.

_____

_____

_____

_____

_____

_____

_____

_____

_____

_____

_____

_____

_____

_____

_____

_____

_____

My day started poorly. Last night I forgot to <u>increase the volume on</u> my radio alarm clock. So this morning I <u>opened my eyes after I slept</u> late. I <u>dressed myself quickly in</u> my clothes and ran to catch the bus. I was in such a hurry that I <u>entered</u> the wrong bus. The bus went several blocks before I realized my mistake. I <u>left</u> the bus and then I tried to <u>solve the problem of</u> how to get to the right bus. Luckily, while I was standing there I <u>met</u> one of my co-workers <u>by chance</u>. He offered to give me a ride to work. I gladly accepted. I <u>entered</u> his car. In the end I got to work on time.

_____

_____

_____

_____

_____

_____

_____

_____

_____

_____

_____

_____

_____

Rewrite the stories from Exercise 4. This time separate the phrasal verbs, if possible.

EXAMPLE:   The house was a mess. Hazel put her apron on.

_____

_____

_____

_____

_____

_____

_____

_____

_____

_____

_____

_____

_____

_____

_____

_____

_____

_____

_____

_____

_____

_____

**Ask your partner questions about the manners of people in his or her country using phrasal verbs.**

EXAMPLE:    men stand when women enter a room

**A:** *In your country, do men stand up when women come into a room?*

**B:** *Yes, they do.*

1. men stand when women enter a room

2. people usually eat in a restaurant

3. people cross their legs when they sit

4. children do household chores when they get older

5. people usually appear at parties one or two hours late

6. call a repairman when appliances stop working

7. return to the same place for vacation each year

8. knock before they enter a room

**Choose the *one* word or phrase that best completes each sentence.**

1. My dog can do many tricks, but there are some things he can't do by _____.
   - (A) itself
   - (B) himself
   - (C) herself
   - (D) myself

2. Are you thirsty? There's some lemonade in the refrigerator. Help _____.
   - (A) myself
   - (B) himself
   - (C) theirselves
   - (D) yourself

3. She fell off the skateboard and hurt _____.
   - (A) by herself
   - (B) by sheself
   - (C) herself
   - (D) sheself

4. Neither boy said who broke the window. They blamed _____.
   - (A) themselves
   - (B) himself
   - (C) each other
   - (D) themself

5. The dance was great. We enjoyed _____.
   - (A) usselves
   - (B) ourselves
   - (C) ourself
   - (D) weself

6. I don't think you can finish that book by yourself. _____ need some help.
   - (A) Will you
   - (B) You're going to
   - (C) You going
   - (D) You are going

7. _____ win the prize for the best actor?
   - (A) Who will
   - (B) Will
   - (C) When will
   - (D) Why you will

8. The almanac predicts that _____ a hurricane in August.
   - (A) there is
   - (B) it will
   - (C) there will be
   - (D) there was

9. What a beautiful morning! I feel great! This _____ a great day!
   - (A) is going to be
   - (B) will be
   - (C) is going being
   - (D) won't be

**10.** I _____ clean up after you. You must clean your own mess.
  (A) am going to
  (B) amn't going to
  (C) 'm not going to
  (D) isn't going to

**11.** _____ study in the library today? No, _____.
  (A) Are you going to...we're not
  (B) Are you going...I'm not
  (C) Do you will...we won't
  (D) Are you going to...I am

**12.** Don't get too excited. Please _____.
  (A) calm yourself
  (B) calm down
  (C) calm
  (D) calm in

**13.** How _____ to get to Ohio next week?
  (A) he go
  (B) are he going
  (C) does he go
  (D) is he going

**14.** _____ we are going to my sister's graduation ceremony.
  (A) Nowadays
  (B) Usually
  (C) A week from today
  (D) Last week

**15.** First she will _____ some papers.
  (A) fill in
  (B) fill
  (C) fill out
  (D) fills

**Identify the *one* underlined word or phrase that must be changed for the sentence to be grammatically correct.**

**16.** Will have you time to go shopping for some groceries tomorrow?
        A              B                    C       D

**17.** Will you throw up this trash before you go upstairs?
        A       B                  C       D

**18.** We're going to clean out the town this weekend.
        A       B          C

**19.** George is going to hand out the trash bags and I'm going to get some volunteers.
              A    B        C                              D

**20.** Please come in. You can take your coat. I'll hang it up.
               A                 B              C    D

**21.** If you fall down, don't worry. Just calm and get up.
               A          B               C        D

**22.** Be careful! Your going to run into that car.
        A          B    C        D

**23.** You're going to have to grow up and learn how to put over your clothes by yourself.
        A      B                                        C                    D

**24.** <u>He's not</u> <u>going to</u> <u>believe</u> this, but I forgot to <u>get up</u> his trash.
        **A**       **B**     **C**                   **D**

**25.** I <u>won't have</u> any fun this weekend. <u>I'm</u> <u>going go to</u> the beach by <u>myself</u>.
         **A**                       **B**   **C**             **D**

**26.** <u>What</u> <u>are you</u> <u>going do</u>? <u>Are you going to</u> write something?
        **A**    **B**      **C**       **D**

**27.** No, <u>I'm no going</u> <u>to write</u>; <u>I'm going</u> to draw <u>some</u> pictures.
              **A**       **B**      **C**        **D**

**28.** What kind of pictures do you draw? I draw pictures <u>of fruit</u>. <u>Will you</u> <u>draws</u> a picture for
                                                           **A**       **B**   **C**

me? Sure, I'll get <u>some pencils</u>.
                 **D**

**29.** <u>What are you</u> <u>going to do</u> this summer? I don't know. I <u>amn't</u> <u>going to go on</u> a vacation.
         **A**           **B**                             **C**      **D**

**30.** <u>That's too bad</u>! <u>You are</u> <u>going to get</u> a chance to <u>get away</u> on weekends?
        **A**           **B**     **C**             **D**

# UNIT

## 22 Comparison with Adjectives

Use the following adjectives to compare the shoes of Bob the basketball player and Felicia the fashion model.

comfortable, dressy, expensive, new, old, casual, big

EXAMPLE: ___Bob's shoes are more___
___comfortable than Felicia's shoes.___

1. _____

2. _____

3. _____

4. _____

5. _____

6. _____

**Bob likes comedy movies and Felicia likes romances. Use the following adjectives to compare the two kinds of movies.**

emotional, exciting, sensitive, sad, funny, silly

7. _____

_____

8. _____

_____

9. _____

_____

10. _____

_____

11. _____

_____

12. _____

_____

---

**EXERCISE 2**   (*Focus 1*)

My hometown is Skagway, Alaska. It is a small, isolated town—only 500 people live there, but the people are very friendly because they all know each other. The town closest to Skagway is 50 miles away.

Skagway is a historic town. In 1898, Skagway was a gold rush town. At that time, 20,000 people lived there. Most of the buildings from that time are still standing. Every summer thousands of tourists visit Skagway to see both a gold rush town and the spectacular beauty of the surrounding mountains.

In the winter Skagway doesn't have many tourists. It is very cold, wet, snowy, and windy, but in the summer the weather is pleasant. Because Skagway is near the Arctic Circle, the days are long. Sometimes the sun never sets at all.

**Using the cues, write sentences comparing your hometown to Skagway.**

EXAMPLE: _The winter weather in Miami is better than in Skagway._

1. good winter weather _____
   _____

2. old _____
   _____

3. far _____
   _____

4. large _____
   _____

5. historic _____
   _____

6. touristy _____
   _____

7. beautiful _____
   _____

8. cold _____
   _____

9. wet _____
   _____

10. snowy _____
    _____

11. windy _____
    _____

12. long days _____
    _____

13. bad winter weather _____
    _____

## EXERCISE 3 (Focus 2)

Bring pictures of your hometown or city to class. Compare the place you are from with those of your classmates. Tell what you think is better or worse about the place you are from.

**Interview your partner. Ask yes/no questions or *who*, *which*, and *whose* questions. Compare the place your partner is from with the place he or she lives now. Use the cues to help you.**

EXAMPLE:   **A:** *Which place is more expensive to live in, Guatemala City or New York?*

**B:** *New York is more expensive.*

OR

**A:** *Is Guatemala City more expensive to live in than New York?*

**B:** *Yes, it is.*

1. expensive

2. crowded

3. small

4. bad traffic

5. clean

6. warm

7. beautiful

8. friendly

9. crime

10. interesting

Sheri is from Iran, but she has lived in the United States for two years. Sheri took the personal values inventory, which compares U.S. values with the values of some other countries.

**Look at Sheri's responses to the personal values inventory and write sentences expressing similarities and differences. The first one has been done for you.**

### PERSONAL VALUES INVENTORY

| U.S. Values | Some Other Countries' Values |
|---|---|
| 1. Innovative         X................................................................ Traditional | |
| 2. Action oriented    ...........................................................X "Being" oriented | |
| 3. Individualistic    ...........................................................X Group oriented | |
| 4. Competitive        ...........................................................X Cooperative | |
| 5. Future oriented X................................................................ Past oriented | |

1. _____ *Sheri is as innovative as people from the U.S.* _____

_____

2. _____

_____

3. _____

_____

4. _____

_____

5. _____

_____

# UNIT
# 23 Comparison with Adverbs

## EXERCISE 1 (Focus 1)

What are the differences between boys and girls? Read the questions below. Check the box that shows your opinion for each.

|     |                                  | BOYS | GIRLS |
|-----|----------------------------------|------|-------|
| 1.  | Who plays jokes more often?      | ____ | ____  |
| 2.  | Who works harder?                | ____ | ____  |
| 3.  | Who studies more seriously?      | ____ | ____  |
| 4.  | Who listens more carefully?      | ____ | ____  |
| 5.  | Who gets hurt more often?        | ____ | ____  |
| 6.  | Who acts more calmly?            | ____ | ____  |
| 7.  | Who cries more frequently?       | ____ | ____  |
| 8.  | Who sings more beautifully?      | ____ | ____  |
| 9.  | Who observes more closely?       | ____ | ____  |
| 10. | Who draws more artistically?     | ____ | ____  |

## EXERCISE 2 (Focus 1)

Using your opinions from Exercise 1, write a sentence for each using the comparative forms of the adverbs.

EXAMPLE: *Girls play jokes more often than boys.*

1. _____
2. _____
3. _____
4. _____
5. _____
6. _____

172    Unit 23

7. _____

8. _____

9. _____

10. _____


## EXERCISE 3   (*Focus 2*)

Pia and Dan are twins. Using the cues, write sentences that tell how they are similar or different.

EXAMPLE:  (draw/creative)  <u>*Dan draws as creatively as Pia.*</u>

1. (spell/good) _____

2. (read/quick) _____

3. (write/neat) _____

4. (talk/quiet) _____

5. (answer/polite) _____

**Nathan and Ned are athletes. They are also alike in many ways. Using the cues, write sentences that tell how they are similar or different.**

6. (jump/high) _____

7. (run/fast) _____

8. (throw/far) _____

9. (practice/frequent) _____

10. (practice/hard) _____

Steve is the owner of Water Trails Kayak Club. Cynthia and her daughter Mariah want to join the kayak club, but first Cynthia has to answer a few questions. Read the information card Steve has to fill out and write the questions he asks. The first one has been done for you.

**CLUB MEMBER**

Name _____ Cynthia Schuemann _____

Age _____    **1.** *How old are you?*

Swimming ability _____    **2.** How _____

_____

Kayaking ability _____    **3.** How _____

_____

Number of years kayaking_____    **4.** How_____

_____

How often kayaking planned _____    **5.** How _____

_____

Distance to kayak_____    **6.** How _____

_____

Distance to kayak club from home    **7.** How _____

_____    _____

Length of Membership:    **8.** How _____

_____ 6 months _____ 1 year    _____

Method of payment:    **9.** How _____

_____ check _____ cash    _____

_____ credit card

**RELATED FAMILY MEMBER**

Name _Mariah Schuemann_

Age _____

Swimming ability _____

Kayaking ability _____

Number of years kayaking _____

How often kayaking planned _____

Distance to kayak _____

10. *How old is your daughter?*

11. How _____
    _____

12. How _____
    _____

13. How _____
    _____

14. How _____
    _____

15. How _____
    _____

# UNIT

# 24 Superlatives

## EXERCISE 1 (Focus 1)

**How much do you know about Canada? Match the information below.**

1. _____ the longest river      **A.** Quebec

2. _____ the tallest mountain      **B.** the prime minister

3. _____ the longest waterfall      **C.** the Milk River

4. _____ the largest lake      **D.** the CN tower

5. _____ the biggest city      **E.** Mount Logan

6. _____ the tallest building      **F.** Toronto

7. _____ the oldest city      **G.** the United States

8. _____ the highest government official      **H.** Alert, the Northwest Territories

9. _____ the town that is the farthest north      **I.** Lake Superior

10. _____ the earliest European explorer      **J.** Della Falls

11. _____ the biggest trading partner      **K.** Jacques Cartier

## EXERCISE 2 (Focus 1)

**Using the information from Exercise 1, write five sentences about Canada.**

EXAMPLE: The Milk River is the longest river in Canada.

1. _____

_____

2. _____

_____

3. _____

_____

4. _____

_____

5. _____

_____

## EXERCISE 3  *(Focuses 1 and 2)*

**Think of all the people you know who have each of the following characteristics or abilities. Choose the person who is at the top of the group and write a sentence with the correct form of the superlative. Be careful to spell the superlative correctly.**

EXAMPLES: tall ___*Jim is the tallest in my family.*___

writes neatly ___*Diane writes the most neatly.*___

1. silly _____

_____

2. sleepy _____

_____

3. runs quickly _____

_____

4. helpful_____

_____

5. sleeps lightly _____

_____

6. pleasant _____

_____

7. heavy_____

_____

8. busy_____

_____

9. sad_____

_____

10. drives slowly_____

_____

11. good musician _____

_____

12. graceful dancer _____

_____

13. has blue eyes _____

_____

14. works hard _____

_____

15. drives far _____

_____

## EXERCISE 4 (Focuses 1 and 2)

**Repeat Exercise 3, except this time write the sentence about the person at the *bottom* of your lists for the following categories.**

1. good writer _____

_____

2. shy _____

_____

3. interesting _____

_____

4. busy _____

_____

5. sings well _____

_____

## EXERCISE 5 (Focus 3)

**Use the cues to ask your partner the following questions about his or her native country. Answer each other's questions in complete sentences. Record your partner's answers.**

EXAMPLE:    famous landmarks

**A:** *What is one of the most famous landmarks in your country?*

**B:** The Statue of Liberty is one of the most famous landmarks in my
country.

1. famous landmarks _____

    _____

2. best restaurants _____

    _____

3. most interesting sights _____

    _____

4. least expensive places to shop _____

    _____

5. longest rivers _____

    _____

6. most common foods _____

    _____

7. biggest industries _____

    _____

8. warmest places to visit _____

    _____

9. greatest artists or entertainers _____

    _____

10. best times to visit _____

    _____

11. most beautiful cities _____

    _____

## EXERCISE 6  (Focus 3)

Tell what you learned about your partner's country to the rest of your classmates. If there are students from the same country as your partner, ask them if they agree with your partner's answers.

EXAMPLE:  I learned that one of the longest rivers in Brazil is the Amazon.

UNIT

# 25 Factual Conditionals

## If

---

**EXERCISE 1**  (*Focus 1*)

Read the statements below. If the statement is true, write "T". If the statement is false, write "F" and then rewrite the statement to make it true. The first one has been done for you.

1. __F__ If you mix yellow and red you get green. _____

   ___*If you mix yellow and red you get orange.*_____

2. _____ If you are on the equator, the sun rises and sets at the same time every day. ___

   _____

3. _____ If you don't get enough sleep, you never get sick. _____

   _____

4. _____ If a tadpole grows up, it becomes a butterfly. _____

   _____

5. _____ If you scuba dive under water, you need an oxygen tank. _____

   _____

6. _____ If there are 366 days in a year, it is a leap year. _____ __

   _____

7. _____ If you eat too many fatty foods, you lose weight. _____

   _____

8. _____ If your skin is exposed to too much sun, you get a sunburn. _____

   _____

9. _____ If plants don't have sunlight, they grow faster. _____

   _____

10. _____ If it is winter, ducks migrate. _____

    _____

11. _____ If a surface is smooth, it has less friction than a rough surface. _____

    _____

**Tell what you do habitually in the following situations.**

EXAMPLE:   When you want to be alone

_If I want to be alone, I go to my bedroom_ _____

1. When you want to be alone _____

   _____

2. When you need a quiet place to study _____

   _____

3. Who takes care of you when you are sick? _____

   _____

4. When you want to be with people _____

   _____

5. When you are caught in a heavy rain _____

   _____

6. When you have too much stress in your life _____

   _____

7. When you don't have enough money to buy what you want ____

   _____

8. When you don't feel like cooking dinner _____

   _____

9. When you have a bad day _____

   _____

10. When you get a good grade on a test _____

   _____

## EXERCISE 3 (Focus 2)

### PART A

Think about when you were a teenager. How did your parents treat you in each of the following situations? Complete the statements.

EXAMPLE:  If you came home late

*If I came home late, my parents didn't let me go out again all month.*

1. If you came home late _____

   _____

2. If you got good grades in school _____

   _____

3. If you wanted new clothes _____

   _____

4. If you didn't clean your room _____

   _____

5. If you needed some money _____

   _____

6. If you wanted to go on a date _____

   _____

### PART B

Are you different from your parents? How do you treat your children? (If you don't have children, imagine that you do.)

EXAMPLE:  *If my daughter comes home late, I don't let her watch TV.* _____

7. If your son/daughter comes home late _____

   _____

8. If your son/daughter gets good grades in school _____

   _____

9. If your son/daughter wants new clothes _____

   _____

10. If your son/daughter didn't clean his/her room _____

    _____

11. If your son/daughter needs money _____

    _____

12. If your son/daughter wants to go on a date _____

    _____

# TOEFL®

 **Test Preparation Exercises**
**Units 22–25**

**Choose the *one* word or phrase that best completes each sentence.**

1. _____ take you to drive to work?
   - (A) How does it
   - (B) How long is it
   - (C) How long does it
   - (D) How far does it

2. It depends. If I _____ my house early, it only _____ 30 minutes.
   - (A) leave...takes
   - (B) left...takes
   - (C) am leaving...is taking
   - (D) leave...took

3. If I leave my house by 6:00 A.M., the traffic _____ it is later.
   - (A) isn't as slow
   - (B) isn't as slow as
   - (C) is slower as
   - (D) is slowest

4. At 6:00 A.M. I can drive _____ than at 6:30 because there is less traffic.
   - (A) quick
   - (B) quicker
   - (C) more quickly
   - (D) most quickly

5. The early drivers are nice; they _____ the later drivers.
   - (A) are more polite than
   - (B) drive crazy as
   - (C) don't drive crazy
   - (D) aren't driving polite

6. They also drive _____ than the later drivers do.
   - (A) carefulest
   - (B) carefully
   - (C) most carefully
   - (D) more carefully

7. Also, the early drivers don't yell, and they honk their horns _____.
   - (A) most frequently
   - (B) less frequently
   - (C) frequenter
   - (D) not frequently

8. One of _____ things of all about late drivers is that they don't pay attention.
   - (A) worse
   - (B) the baddest
   - (C) the worst
   - (D) worse than

9. Late drivers put on their make-up or shave while they're driving _____ early drivers.
   - (A) more often
   - (B) more often than
   - (C) the most often
   - (D) more than

10. They are _____ drivers of all.
    (A) more dangerous than      (C) the most dangerous
    (B) the dangerousest          (D) most dangerous

11. Once I saw a man reading while he was driving. I'm sure he was the _____ driver of all.
    (A) most careful              (C) very careful
    (B) least careful             (D) less careful than

12. _____ you have to drive?
    (A) How farther do            (C) How farthest do
    (B) How far                   (D) How far do

13. It's only 18 miles _____ a shortcut.
    (A) whenever I took           (C) if I take
    (B) if I am taking            (D) when taking

14. I know it's the same distance no matter what time I leave, but if I leave later it seems _____ when I leave early.
    (A) farther than              (C) farrer than
    (B) the furthest              (D) far

15. No one at my job travels as far as _____.
    (A) I can                     (C) I do
    (B) I will                    (D) I am


**Identify the *one* underlined word or phrase that must be changed for the sentence to be grammatically correct.**


16. <u>Whenever</u> you <u>fly</u> from Europe to <u>North America</u> you <u>gain</u> time.
    **A**          **B**                    **C**              **D**

17. <u>If</u> it <u>is</u> noon in <u>London,</u> it <u>was</u> 6 A.M. in Montreal.
    **A    B**          **C**          **D**

18. <u>One of the</u> <u>difficultest</u> <u>things</u> about traveling across the Atlantic Ocean <u>is</u> jet lag.
    **A**          **B**          **C**                                                  **D**

19. <u>The</u> <u>good</u> and <u>fastest</u> way to get over jet lag <u>is</u> to plan ahead.
    **A    B**          **C**                              **D**

20. <u>If</u> the time change <u>is</u> <u>more than</u> six hours, your sense of time <u>was</u> distorted.
    **A**              **B**   **C**                                  **D**

21. You will do everything <u>very sleepily</u> during the day, and feel <u>more alert</u> at night.
                              **A      B**                              **C     D**

22. The <u>goodest</u> advice I can give you is to make the change <u>as slowly as</u> possible. Don't try
         **A**                                                    **B**      **C**
    to stay awake if you're <u>very</u> sleepy.
                             **D**

**23.** We must <u>treat</u> ocean resources <u>more</u> <u>thoughtfully</u> <u>that</u> we have in the past.
           **A**                        **B**   **C**    **D**

**24.** Governments need to work <u>more closely</u> with their citizens <u>than</u> they are now. They must
                                   **A**                            **B**

preserve marine life <u>more carefullier</u>.
                   **C**      **D**

**25.** Fishermen <u>are</u> <u>worryier</u> <u>than</u> <u>most people</u> about the condition of the ocean.
                  **A**    **B**    **C**      **D**

**26.** <u>Large groups</u> of fish are <u>least</u> <u>numerous</u> <u>than</u> in the past.
       **A**                   **B**    **C**    **D**

**27.** Ocean pollution <u>ruins</u> life <u>just</u> <u>as effectively</u> <u>than</u> over-fishing.
                  **A**       **B**      **C**     **D**

**28.** Oil spills are <u>biger</u> today <u>than in the past</u>; they pollute oceans <u>more frequently</u> <u>than</u>
                  **A**          **B**                       **C**      **D**
before.

**29.** Concerned citizens are <u>more aware</u> of the problem. They complain <u>loudly</u> <u>than before</u>
                            **A**                        **B**    **C**

about the problems of <u>the oceans</u>.
                       **D**

**30.** They remind us that oceans are <u>just</u> <u>as important today</u> they <u>were</u> <u>in the past</u>.
                                  **A**          **B**         **C**    **D**